Ready-to-Use
Performance Appraisals

READY-TO-USE PERFORMANCE APPRAISALS

Downloadable, Customizable Tools for Better, Faster Reviews!

WILLIAM S. SWAN, Ph.D.

with

LESLIE E. WILSON

John Wiley & Sons, Inc.

ISBN-13: 978-0-470-04709-5

ISBN-10: 0-470-04709-7

Printed in the United States of America.

10   9   8   7   6   5   4   3   2   1

CONTENTS

This introduction includes information about how to download the forms and evaluation statements in this book.

PART I
TIPS FOR EFFECTIVE PERFORMANCE APPRAISALS

This chapter covers guidelines and tips for evaluating performance, including common rating errors and how to avoid them. It also covers how to write the performance appraisal. This includes how to gather and analyze data over the year, how to accurately and fairly determine the individual and overall numerical ratings, and how to write the narrative summary.

This chapter includes practical tips and tools for writing and delivering the performance appraisal. Specific topics in this section include common errors in appraisals and performance objectives.

PART II
DOWNLOADABLE PERFORMANCE APPRAISAL FORMS

This chapter includes a downloadable, model performance appraisal form you can adapt to your organization and circumstances. Each section of the form is described in detail.

This chapter covers deciding on competencies, creating a rating scale, and dealing with your existing form.

CONTENTS

PART III
READY-TO-USE, DOWNLOADABLE, CUSTOMIZABLE EVALUATION STATEMENTS

Tools to Complete or Create an Appraisal Form

Sample Forms from Different Companies

Twenty-One Top Core Competencies

Four Managerial Competencies

How to Use This Book

There are many different needs during the performance management process that draw a reader to this book. You may be confronted with the immediate need to complete your company's performance appraisal form for an employee who reports to you. If so, turn immediately to Part III, "Ready-to-Use Downloadable Evaluation Statements," which is a particularly useful resource for that purpose. It allows you to select, download, and insert into your performance appraisal form evaluation statements that best fit the employee's performance on many core competencies. No matter what issues you are asked to comment on for an employee's performance, you will find relevant statements in one or more of these competency forms. Note that although we have chosen what we consider to be the most common titles for the competencies, it is the content of the evaluation statements that are important. Therefore, readers should not be put off if, for example, we have labeled a competency "Customer Focus" and on their form this competency is called "Client Service." The idea is the same, and the text included in this chapter would be entirely applicable.

For each of the twenty-one core competencies and four managerial competencies, we have provided evaluative statements for three levels of performance: *Exceeded Expectations, Met Expectations,* and *Did Not Meet Expectations.* This provides you with more precise statements to quickly choose, download, and insert onto the employee's form. The narratives are loosely based on a mid-level employee—that is, on someone who is neither extremely junior nor extremely senior. However, the phrasing is general enough that with just a few tweaks, the text could be made applicable to any job level.

Our research has indicated that the most challenging and time-consuming part of completing the performance appraisal form for managers is writing descriptions of an employee's performance against the competencies listed on the form. We therefore carefully selected the most commonly used and universal competencies and provided actual statements you can download, adapt, and use immediately. It is our firm belief that the editing process is much easier than the creation of performance text from scratch. The text provided in this book is meant to be able to be cut and pasted into a performance form and used exactly as is (with minor edits, such as including the employee's name, for instance). We urge you to add specific examples from the employee's behavior during the review period to enrich and personalize the statements. The employee him/herself can and should be a source for these behavioral examples.

At the other end of the reader continuum are human resources professionals (or task force teams) who are asked to create or recommend a new performance appraisal form for their organization. Alternatively, you may be charged with the responsibility to improve an existing form. Part II, Chapter 3, contains a Model Performance Appraisal Form ready to be downloaded and adapted to your organization's needs. We purposely kept the format simple for ease of use by the reader, but you can easily retain the logic and elements of the form, while adding your organization's logo and otherwise designing the visual layout in any way you like. This model form draws on the best-practice aspects of performance management, and the chapter also provides an explanation of each section of the form.

Chapter 4 provides more in-depth information on selecting competencies, choosing a rating scale, and working with your existing form.

Chapter 5 adds examples of actual performance appraisal forms from different companies, so you can compare and contrast the approaches used. Integrating a particularly relevant concept from Chapter 4 into your modification of the model form from Chapter 3 might be a successful strategy.

Finally, there are the readers who have direct reports or employees, and who are seeking to understand the performance management process for their own use, or for their organization. Traditionally, the members of this group are identified as corporate managers and supervisors. However, any small business owner, physician, dentist, architect, optometrist, lawyer, or real estate broker who has at least one employee or associate also needs to manage that person's performance. For this larger audience, the entire book, starting with Part I, provides a good overview of the landscape of managing performance. The tools and forms throughout the book will prove helpful as well. Additionally, the evaluation statements provided in Part III could be downloaded by anyone who needs to provide feedback on an employee, thus making them appropriate for peer or stakeholder reviews as well. In fact, the text provided in this section can be used by practically any audience and in any feedback setting—from mid-year to project-based to year-end feedback, and for both written forms and for quick ideas for verbal feedback sessions.

This book provides practical, user-friendly ready-resource tools to assist you in completing a performance appraisal form or in developing a form. For a more complete treatment of the performance management process, including details on how to conduct the annual performance appraisal session, set measurable objectives, and create a development plan, we refer you to Dr. Swan's book *How to Do a Superior Performance Appraisal* (New York: John Wiley & Sons, 1991).

Also, we are always looking to add to and improve the resources and tools offered in this book. If, for example, you have any suggestions for additional competencies or language for the current competencies, let us know, and we will consider them for the next edition. Suggestions can be sent to: info@swanconsultants.com.

How to Download the Forms and Evaluation Statements in This Book

Visit the Wiley web site at www.wiley.com/go/PerformanceAppraisalForms. Use the product search window tool to search by title or author, and when you find this book, follow the instructions there for downloading material.

Ready-to-Use
Performance Appraisals

PART I

TIPS FOR
EFFECTIVE PERFORMANCE
APPRAISALS

CHAPTER 1

Guidelines and Tips for Rating Performance

When we speak of *rating performance*, we are not referring merely to the clerical exercise of checking off boxes and averaging numbers, but also to the crucial business of arriving at sound judgments based on the evidence accumulated over the entire appraisal period. It is a task that requires managers to be fair and objective, and for most people, there is the rub. As a human being and not a robot, all your judgments are to some degree subjective. If there is no evidence to support or contradict your judgment, it is that much harder to know when you are wrong.

Common Rating Errors

In an effort to cope with this problem, industrial psychologists interested in how ratings are done for performance appraisals have categorized the 10 most common rating errors. As you read them, think about which errors you may have observed or of which you may have been a victim.

1. Similar to Me

Tending to rate people higher if they are similar to you (have the same values, interests, preferences), or rating them lower if they are not similar to you

Although this may sound like the behavior of snobs and aristocrats, it is a serious problem in a workforce characterized by increasing diversity, in which some managers cannot relate to the cultural differences of their employees.

2. Positive Leniency

Rating higher than a person deserves

"I give high ratings. It motivates my employees, it makes them feel good." This approach usually takes the form of giving Bob a higher rating than he deserves to encourage him, hoping he will do better next year. However, Mark and Susan, who work in the same unit, receive the rating they actually deserve. When they see Bob getting a rating as high as theirs although it is obvious to them that he does not deserve it, they may be demoralized and discouraged. And what do you do next year when Bob *does not* improve? He can argue that his performance did not change from last year, so why should he get a lower rating? In fact being rated higher than one deserves is actually demotivating ("I can get the rating without working for it") and fosters disrespect for the process. This rater error is particularly common if the rater is rushed.

3. Negative Leniency

Being reluctant to assign high ratings to individuals; rating people lower than they deserve

"Nobody's perfect." This is another strong tendency if the rater is rushed. Some managers set unattainable goals and objectives; thus, high ratings are never possible. Others are strict graders and refuse to give a rating at the top of the scale.

4. Halo-or-Horns Effect

Being overly influenced by a single favorable or unfavorable trait that colors the judgment of the individual's other traits

Alternatively, prior to the review, the manager may allow another person's positive or negative evaluation to affect the rating of the employee.

Jeff had incredible success in the past. Now it seems that he can do no wrong. Conversely, Jeanne had an off year two years ago. Her current high-quality performance is diminished by the memory of two years ago.

5. Recency Effect

Rating someone down or up based solely on recent events; ignoring the performance of the entire period

"What have you done for me lately?"

This is especially likely when the manager has not been keeping records during the year. Recent behavior and performance seem more relevant and meaningful, even if we remember the earlier performance.

6. Attribution Bias

Tending to see poor performance more within the control of the individual, and to see superior performance as more influenced by external factors

This sounds academic at first glance, but you are probably quite familiar with it. "If Steve is successful, it's because of me. If he is not successful, it's his fault." (Of course, perhaps I did not coach him enough, set clear enough goals, or check back often enough.)

7. Stereotyping

Generalizing across a group; not recognizing individual differences

Beyond the obvious gender, racial, or cultural assumptions sometimes made, I run across managers who assume all college graduates with a 3.9 grade point average make the best job candidates, all engineers can learn quickly, all research scientists are highly analytical, and all salespeople are motivated and ambitious.

8. Contrast Effect

Making comparisons; evaluating the employee relative to the person last evaluated

This is most often seen with teachers or professors who rip to shreds the first student's essay, only to realize by the fourth or fifth paper that every student seems to be missing the point: All the papers that come *after* that realization are treated much more leniently.

9. First Impression

Forming an initial positive or negative judgment and then ignoring or distorting subsequent information to avoid changing the initial impression

While similar to the halo-or-horns effect, here the rater actually is unable to shake an initial impression or admit a mistaken perception. This phenomenon has caused many a personal relationship to drag on longer than the objective evidence would support.

10. Central Tendency

Placing people in the middle of the scale, or close to the midpoint to avoid extreme positions; playing safe

Some organizations have actually forced managers to make this error by requiring a forced distribution or rating across employees to resolve a clustering of ratings at the top of the scale. Grade inflation should be corrected, but forced distribution is a draconian solution.

There is no way to eliminate the subjective element from judgments about employee performance. If managers have a mountain of facts at their disposal, their chances of being objective are greater than if they only have a few. But managers still have to interpret those facts and decide which ones are the most meaningful.

Nevertheless, good documentation and a systematic approach can make managers right a much greater percentage of the time. At the very least, it can make all their decisions defendable: The facts and procedures prove that judgments were not made arbitrarily. For that matter, systematic documentation and evaluation also can give other people the opportunity to look at that same data and come to their own conclusions. This can be important if upper management's input and approval are required.

Writing the Performance Appraisal

In this chapter, we discuss writing the appraisal as if you are using a variation of the Model Performance Appraisal Form that we present in Chapter 3 (Form 3.1). You will find it useful even if you cannot employ all the steps in our version of the form. The principles of writing an accurate and effective performance appraisal are the same whatever form you use.

It is a three-step process:

1. Gather and analyze data throughout the appraisal period.
2. Rate the performance.
3. Write the narrative portion of the appraisal.

Of these three tasks, the first is by far the most time consuming and complex. It is also the most crucial.

Gather and Analyze Data throughout the Appraisal Period

If a manager wants to avoid the recency effect among other common errors, this is really the only way. Yet for many supervisors, it seems to be the most difficult to square with the realities of everyday management. "Where do I find the time?" Much depends on the degree of contact between manager and employees. How often does the manager really see the employees doing what they do?

Collect Data at Regular Intervals

The manager must determine in advance the time span within which data will be collected throughout the appraisal period—and then, when the time comes, do it. You might think of these as periodic *miniappraisals,* although the manager is only collecting information to use for ongoing coaching and feedback, not for final conclusions.

The appropriate time schedule for some may be weekly, for others monthly, quarterly, or semiannually, depending on the degree of involvement with the employee and the employee's responsibilities. On the one hand, Phil, who is responsible for purchasing, selecting, and installing equipment, also must maintain the efficiency of the area and achieve these goals through teams reporting to him. The complexity and the high degree of independence inherent in Phil's responsibilities might warrant relatively infrequent miniappraisals, perhaps done quarterly. On the other hand, Phil can and should collect information on *his* employees with much greater frequency—their tasks are simpler and more numerous; there is more data to collect.

Most managers are alert to relevant information when it hits their desk. They may even request certain reports or documents regularly. The problem with this approach is that it does not ensure that they are tracking each objective or performance factor regularly. At the end of the year, many gaps may exist in the data. We are suggesting a more systematic approach.

Assume a manager has decided that a monthly interval is appropriate. At each interval, the manager should see if he or she has information relevant to each of the performance objectives and performance factors. If not, the manager should check over the past month to see if anything has happened that should have been documented but was not. If the answer is no, then the manager should pay particular attention in the coming month to collecting data that will fill in the gaps.

If by the end of the year there is no information against an objective, how can the manager evaluate it? The goal is to have a number of pieces of information on each objective and performance factor by the end of the appraisal period.

Some managers ask the employee to give them the information relating to the objectives or performance factors in a monthly report. That is an excellent idea, but by itself is not enough. Unless the manager imposes an extremely high degree of organization and structure on it, the report will probably not cover all the performance objectives and all the performance factors, and the manager needs information on all of them. The discipline is to search actively and regularly, throughout the year, for the information on each objective and performance factor.

Do It Openly and without Pressure

We are not suggesting that a manager stand behind a pole, watch the employees, and take notes while they are working. Managers should avoid giving employees the feeling that they are being watched and judged. They should be able to say something like this: "Linda, these are the things we've agreed on for next year. We may make some adjustments during the course of the year, but for the moment, this is our target. At the end of this year, my overall evaluation of your performance will be based on how well you have done on all these individual issues. To assure I have enough information to make that judgment, I am going to be making notes to myself regarding all these issues on a regular basis. But, there is something you can do to help me. I'd like you to give me information on these issues as they come up, so I'll have accurate information and can make a fair assessment at the end of the year."

Is Linda going to run to her manager with every little mistake she makes? Perhaps not. But you would be surprised how many times an employee who understands the basis for the evaluation will go to the manager and say, "Well, I know you're going to hear about this anyway, but I want to give you my side of it." Or, "Here's something that's happening that isn't going so smoothly, I want to make sure there isn't any misunderstanding regarding the approach I'm about to take." It adds clarity for you to ask for employees' input. Experience shows that employees are often harsher on themselves than their managers would have been.

Document as You Give Feedback during the Year

If data collected six weeks into the year suggests that employees are veering down the wrong path, it would be unwise to wait until the end of the year to tell them about it. The manager should make an intervention now, if possible. On the other hand, that event, and the action the manager finds necessary to take, should still go into the system as a piece of data for ultimate inclusion in the performance appraisal.

Suppose I am reviewing Linda's performance at the end of the year. She says, "Lately I've been trying hard and doing a lot better. I think I deserve a rating of 'exceeded the standard' on that performance factor." The manager can say, "In fact, most of the year your performance on that factor 'met the standard' and a couple of times you exceeded it. But in the first two months, you were performing 'below the standard' so overall for the year you performed at 'met the standard.'" Certainly it's encouraging that Linda's performance is improving. But the evaluation period is the entire year, not just the past two months.

What Kind of Data to Gather

There are three types of information that a manager should gather with reference to employees' performance: objective data, significant incidents, and observations:

Objective data: Only the manager is in a position to know what kinds of objective data are available on the employees. For sales representatives, perhaps there are call reports, listings, dollar volume of sales, number of calls per day, or quarterly reports (did the employee get them in on time?). For information technology professionals, there may be project milestones or deadlines. For any role, there may be quantifiable information that is directly a result of their individual efforts. Whatever objective data exists should be taken into account.

Significant incidents: Throughout the year, as they happen, record events that stand out. We call them *significant* instead of critical to underline that the manager should not merely be recording negative information. A manager should also record positive events that relate to the performance objectives or performance factors.

The manager may not have many significant incidents on each employee, but even a few can be very informative; and a single significant incident can contain evidence for more than one performance factor or performance objective. Suppose mine is a consumer products company: In the middle of the appraisal period, the release date is set for a new product; an advertising campaign is organized; and a manufacturing facility is ready to gear up. At the last minute, my employee Alison discovers that computer-manufacturing software my company planned to supply to the manufacturing group will not be available from the supplier on time. She examines the options: (1) reworking the manufacturing standards, (2) finding another supplier of another program, or (3) arranging for partial shipment. She chooses the third option, which works out well.

That is a complex accomplishment, and it tells a lot about the way Alison works. Through this significant incident, she has demonstrated some degree of initiative, an analytical approach to problem solving, and her command of her technical arena or knowledge. So, for her performance appraisal, that one incident can supply information on all three of those performance factors.

Behaviors you observe as you manage: The third category consists of behaviors the manager observes when "managing by walking around." I pick up many problems about my own company by asking, "Why is that done that way?" So if while managing by walking around, a manager notices something relevant to performance (not necessarily that the employees are sitting around reading the newspaper), make a note of it.

Have a Record-Keeping System

If, because it would take too much time, you resisted our suggestion to talk to the employee prior to the performance appraisal, then you are probably saying, "Record-keeping system? Here we go again." Record keeping, however, need not be very elaborate or time-consuming.

If I have just one or two employees, then it might be possible for me to keep my records of employee performance in whatever regular appointment or scheduling software or book I use—week-at-a-glance, month-at-a-glance, or just a daily schedule book.

The preceding situation is probably an exception. At some point, most managers have to gather data on many individuals at once. They undoubtedly have a file folder for each individual, thus making record keeping even easier. On a periodic basis, the manager takes the little notes that have accumulated on the employees, dates them individually, and dumps each note into the respective employee's file folder.

By the end of the appraisal period, the file folder should have a number of pieces of paper relevant to that employee's performance. The dating automatically confers a certain order on the collection. The manager increases the order by separating out all papers that are associated with objective number one. In other words, the manager would say, "Well, what's my evidence for performance objective number one?" Not "What do I remember, what do I think of, how do I think this person did, do I like this person?" but "What information do I have?"

If I, as manager, have only two pieces of paper relevant to that objective, I am in trouble. If I have several pieces of paper, plus a critical incident or two, some pieces of observed behavior, several objective pieces of data, perhaps some information I've gotten directly from the employee, I can say with confidence, "Well, obviously the evidence supports the conclusion this person overall is 'meeting the standard' I set," or "I can see plenty of evidence that this employee is way above [or way below] the standard." Whatever my conclusion may be, the evidence is there.

I will have that evidence if I throw it into the file folder on a regular basis. If I develop the discipline of making notes to myself on a regular basis and putting them in the file folder, my task at the end of the year will be much easier. In fact, it can take some of the pressure off me during the year, because I know I need not remember every item relevant to every employee's performance. Once I have added a note to the file, I can stop worrying about it.

Rating the Performance

The manager who has gathered information regularly during the year and has a reasonably well-organized record-keeping system is ready to rate the performance on the appraisal form. First, the manager will rate each objective, then each performance factor, and finally give an overall or summary rating.

Here are some rules of thumb for avoiding those common rater errors described at the outset of this chapter.

- Know the standards.
- Stick to those standards.
- Describe specific facts in the narrative.
- Document, document, document.
- Use multiple miniappraisals.

Know the Standards

Whether managers are using the formal performance objectives and performance factors put forward in Chapter 3, they need to know as precisely as they can against what standard they are measuring employees.

Stick to Those Standards

This is not a restatement of the first rule. Many managers, when they get to this point, throw out the requirements while knowing very well what they are. They say, "Oh, George is doing so well, trying so hard, I think I'll rate him as having 'Fully Met Expectation' even though, technically, he deserves a 'Did Not Meet Expectation,' because, I don't know, I don't want to have an argument with him." Do not do that. If George knows what the standards are and he has been coached well during the year, the final rating should not be a surprise to him. In any case, occasionally presenting reality to an employee is part of a manager's job. Arguments can be avoided by other means than unconditional surrender.

Describe Specific Facts in the Narrative

Probably, several people are going to read this document, including upper management and perhaps one or more individuals in the human resources department. One of the things they are going to look for is whether there is a reasonable correspondence between the narrative and the rating. Another reader of this document will be the employee: Making it clear, in the narrative explanation, how the rating was arrived at will greatly reduce the occasions for disagreement or resistance.

Document, Document, Document

This is the performance appraisal equivalent of the "location, location, location" message you hear about real estate. With proper documentation, ratings are more accurate because the manager has enough data to reach meaningful conclusions. One might argue about individual facts, but the overall impression is obviously based on the preponderance of evidence.

Not only is this important for the accuracy and defensibility of the appraisal, it is also crucial for employee feedback. Employees' cooperation with plans for problem solving depends on the manager's ability to convince them that problems really exist. Say an employee differs with my conclusion, and I know of seven instances in which the employee failed to meet the standard of performance. The employee might say of one of these instances: "Well, I'm not sure that incident means what you think it means." I can then say, "Okay, but if I forget about that one, what about the other six instances. There seems to be a clear pattern here."

Use Multiple Miniappraisals

Not all managers have direct contact with each of their employees on a daily basis. There may be someone between them. If so, then that person can give the manager additional data. This middle person should be told what the requirements, standards, or expectations are and what information he should be looking for. He should gather the information on a weekly or a monthly basis and give it to the manager as part of the overall information-gathering process. In organizations that use matrix management, an employee may have four or five managers in the course of a year. In information technology departments and the comptroller/audit department, a person often works on multiple team engagements or assignments, so there are multiple sources of input. All this data can be pooled at the end of the year and used for the performance appraisal.

Giving Grades

A manager should not emphasize the numerical score an employee receives with respect to a given performance factor or performance objective: We suggest that managers say "met the standard" or "occasionally exceeded the standard" rather than "I've given you a 3" or "I've given you a 4." It is the best approach to use when managing and improving employee performance.

Determining the Overall Rating

The fact remains, however, that to arrive at an overall rating that will enable a manager to compare the overall performance of different employees or compare a given employee's overall performance this year and last year, the manager needs to translate these phrases into numbers.

This is the point at which most performance appraisal systems fall apart. The overall rating may seem to those who receive it a somewhat mystical interpretation of the individual scores. It is often difficult to arrive at and still more difficult to defend. But it need not be. If you follow the performance appraisal methods we present in this book, we can show you how to arrive at an overall rating that is easy to calculate and meaningful in a way that each participant can easily appreciate.

It all hinges on the issue of weighting. A manager must have some way of expressing the relative importance and difficulty of the employee's different responsibilities. Therefore, at the beginning of the appraisal period, a manager should assign weights to each of the performance objectives and each of the performance factors. Each is given a certain percentage; all the percentages for the performance objectives add up to 100 percent, as do the percentages for the performance factors. It is important that managers explain this system fully to employees, so they understand where to put their greatest efforts, and so the ultimate evaluation does not come as a shock.

For example, at the beginning of the year, the manager would tell Fred, the employee, what percentage each of the performance objectives would be worth; the manager might even negotiate the values with Fred. Of the six objectives, say the first objective represented 30 percent, the second represented 30 percent, and the remaining four represented 10 percent each. Those first two objectives, then, represented 60 percent of the total objectives. If Fred's performance was below standard on those two objectives, that fact would weigh heavily on his appraisal even if he achieved perfection with respect to the remaining objectives.

The manager would not need to rely on what is obvious, or on the general sense of how things stack up. Once the manager arrived at a decision about the employee's performance on each objective, she would calculate the final result with a glance at the Performance Rating Analysis Worksheet (Form 1.1) found, in downloadable form, at the end of this chapter.

As the form suggests, the manager would start by listing the objectives, then under the "Enter Weight" column, she would note the weight that she assigned these objectives with the agreement of the employee, at the beginning of the year. Next, she would circle the rating she gave the employee's performance of the objective. For each objective, she would multiply the weight (i.e., the percentage point) times the number representing the rating and note that in the column to the right. She would add the "Combined Score" column and divide by 100 to derive my figure for the overall weighted-average rating for objectives.

Then the manager would go through the same process for the performance factors; these too can be weighted (although the manager can give them all equal weight if she feels that expresses the truth about the job). This will yield a weighted average rating for performance factors.

Finally, the manager would need to repeat the process one more time. If she has decided that Part I of the Model Performance Appraisal Form in Chapter 3 (the performance objectives) and Part II (the performance factors) are of equal weight, then Part III, the overall summary rating, is a simple average of the two previous weighted averages. If these are weighted unequally (as they usually are), the manager again multiplies the weighted rating for performance objectives and for performance factors against their respective weightings, add the sum and divide by 100. The final number will need to be rounded off, with one decimal point allowed (e.g., 3.9 on a 5-point scale).

On the one hand, we might determine that for Bob, his objective (sales success as shown in dollar volume) represents 90 percent of his job, in which case his performance factors would represent 10 percent. Barring any unethical behavior, the manager has decided that she is less concerned about how he achieved his goals than whether he achieved them. On the other hand, for Brian's job the objectives may represent only 50 percent of the job; his ongoing day-to-day behavior is just as important as his objectives.

In both cases, let us repeat, it is important that the employees be fully aware of different weights given their different responsibilities at the beginning of the appraisal period.

When a manager finally comes to the overall rating (Part III of Form 3.1) and someone says, "Why did you give me this rating?" the manager can say, "Well, this is how I evaluated you on your total objectives; this is how I evaluated you on all your performance factors. Now because, as we have agreed, the objectives were a larger portion of the job, they have been weighted more heavily. Therefore, the overall rating for this performance appraisal is that you met the standard." The same logic and the same explanation apply when employees question their rating in total performance factors or total performance objectives. "I've rated you as performing above the standard for your last three performance objectives: but you'll remember we agreed that the first objective was as important as the other three combined, and on that objective you were Below Expectation, so on balance I'm rating you as having Fully Met Expectation."

This method of rating still requires judgment and has subjective aspects (it is impossible to entirely eliminate the subjective element) but it is defendable, reasonable, provides a consistent basis of comparison between employees, and connects back to the actual job-relevant events of the year. From the data gathered throughout the year, a manager can produce evidence in support of every item. It is certainly light years away from the usual statement of "it seems to me that overall you're doing okay, so I've rated you as 'meeting the standard.'"

The Narrative Portion of the Appraisal

The narrative portion of the appraisal is a summary of the best information collected on each objective and performance factor. It is the place where managers present their evidence and reasoning for the conclusions expressed by the rating. A manager should write at least one or two sentences of narrative for each performance objective and performance factor. Here are some rules to remember when writing a narrative.

Highlight the Best Evidence

For any individual item, managers should highlight their best evidence. If you have 10 pieces of information for a particular issue, 4 or 5 may be incontrovertible. Others may leave some room for interpretation, argument, and discussion. In the written appraisal, managers should highlight the most defendable evidence or information, saving the rest for the face-to-face discussion.

Give Comparison Basis for Qualitative Data

Generally a manager should compare the employee's performance to the standard—not to the performance of any other given individual (e.g., Bob has not shown as much initiative as Mary). Not only does this create bad feelings when this appraisal is shown to the employee, it is a statistically invalid way of measuring performance. However, a manager can and should point out that the standard for "initiative," as defined for that job is one that the other employees holding the same position in the organization have easily met or exceeded during this appraisal period and in the past. This is an effective way to deal with an employee's contention that the standard is set too high.

Give More Evidence for Especially High and Low Ratings

It is inevitable that your manager and senior management will give closer, more careful scrutiny to the extreme ratings: the highs and the lows. Therefore, managers should take extra care that they have (and that they present) all the data they need to back up those ratings. If there is ever arbitration or any other outside scrutiny of an employee's performance, those ratings will be studied in more detail, so managers certainly want to make sure that they justify them. In recognition of this fact, many organizations' forms *require* a narrative statement for ratings at the top and bottom of the scale. This encourages the rater error of central tendency because midpoint ratings do not require the extra effort of a narrative statement. We recommend narrative statements for *all* the performance objectives and performance factors, with special attention to very high and very low ratings.

Use Language Consistent with Your Form

Managers should use language in the narrative that is consistent with the form, so that anyone looking at the appraisal can easily relate the rating scale to the narrative and can see how they reinforce each other. Furthermore, by keeping the language of the narrative consistent with the rating scale, the manager is also keeping the language of all the employees' narratives consistent with each other.

    If the midpoint of the rating scale is "achieved established standards" in the language of a form, the manager should not write in the narrative, "did okay" or "performed about average." If the employee achieved the top of the rating scale on a particular objective, "did exceedingly well," or "did great in my book," or "one of the best I've seen this year" just doesn't make sense. Instead the manager should say something like, "On this particular objective I feel that Bill surpassed the established standards regularly." Consistent language supports a manager's arguments and makes the overall rating clearer and more defendable.

Be Careful of Giving Assurances or Making Promises

It can be dangerous to make categorical promises in exchange for performance improvements unless managers are sure they can back them up; courts have ruled that there is an implied contract in such statements. If a manager tells Janet, "Make 150 percent of your quota next year and you'll be in line to be supervisor!" and Janet meets her quota but there are no openings for supervisor, the company and the manager may be in trouble. Legalities aside, it is never a good idea to create misunderstandings with employees. Therefore, managers should be careful to word statements in a way that is consistent with reality. Managers can suggest the possibility of advancement or reward, if such possibilities exist, but all the "ifs" need to be included. "Were you to achieve this level, you'd be eligible for possible advancement if there were such opportunities."

PERFORMANCE RATING WORKSHEET*
Downloadable Form 1.1

This form allows you to convert your individual ratings into an overall rating that is meaningful. Use this form three times:

1. To calculate weighted rating for all objectives.
2. To calculate weighted rating for all performance factors.
3. To determine the combined weighted rating for objectives and performance factors.

Weight Definitions:

Adjust the weight for each criterion based on its level of importance for successful job performance. Be sure the total adds up to 100%.

Rating Definitions:

5 = Greatly Exceeded Expectation   2 = Did Not Meet Expectation

4 = Consistently Exceeded Expectation   1 = Significantly Below Expectation

3 = Fully Met Expectation

List Objectives or Performance Factors	Enter Weight	Circle Rating High-Low	Combined Score (Weight X Rating)
1.		5 4 3 2 1	
2.		5 4 3 2 1	
3.		5 4 3 2 1	
4.		5 4 3 2 1	
5.		5 4 3 2 1	
6.		5 4 3 2 1	
7.		5 4 3 2 1	
8.		5 4 3 2 1	
(Total Weight must equal 100%)	(100%)		Total Combined Scores:

Divide "Total Combined Scores" by 100 for overall weighted rating: _____ = _____ ÷ 100

For Part III of Model Performance Appraisal Form:

Overall Weighted Rating, combining weighted scores on
Objectives and Performance Factors: (include one decimal point) _____

1.0–1.9   2.0–2.9   3.0–3.9   4.0–4.5   4.5–5.0

CHAPTER 2

The Face-to-Face Meeting: How to Deliver an Appraisal to an Employee

Apart from the strengths and weaknesses inherent in a given performance appraisal system, errors of implementation can occur no matter what techniques you use. In fact, the way your performance appraisal system is administered and the training given to the managers who use it probably have more to do with the effectiveness of the appraisal than any other factors. Some performance appraisal systems prevent or reduce these errors more than others, but all are subject to some of them.

The eight most common appraisal errors are:

1. Inadequately defined standards of performance
2. Overemphasis on recent performance
3. Reliance on gut feelings
4. Employee's miscomprehension of performance expectations
5. Insufficient or unclear performance documentation
6. Inadequate time allotment for the discussion
7. Too much talking by manager/supervisor
8. Lack of a follow-up plan

Inadequately Defined Standards of Performance

Whatever we call it—the standard or the definition of quality—what is expected must be defined in advance if the performance appraisal is to have any meaning for the employee, for the organization, and for the rating manager.

If at the end of the year of managing a person, suppose a manager says to that individual, "I don't think you're trying hard enough." The employee could reply, "Compared to what? What was the standard against which you held me? How do I know what you expect of me? If I was performing up to the standard, how would you know it, and how could I prove it?"

If a manager can't answer those questions, he doesn't just have a disgruntled employee, he has a potentially invalid performance appraisal. A clear and measurable idea of effective or superior job performance is the indispensable basis for any performance appraisal. Yet, all too often, it's missing. Managers need to know what they expect of their employees, otherwise evaluations can't be made or defended at the end of the appraisal period.

Overemphasis on Recent Performance

If a manager isn't gathering data over the appraisal period, inevitably, whatever happened in the beginning tends to get pushed back further and further into memory, and he or she winds up basing the appraisal on the events of the most recent month or two. Some of you are familiar with this as the "Christmas phenomenon": Service providers as well as children tend to be more attentive and on their best behavior right around Christmastime, when they know they're being evaluated. Well, employees know the same thing. A month or two prior to their appraisal they're likely to be on their best behavior. They make lots of suggestions, come in on time, and tend to be responsive to suggestions.

It may seem like an obvious ploy, but it works. It is not just that the manager tends to forget what happened more than a few months ago, it is also a matter of wishful thinking. Maybe there was a problem with this employee's performance earlier in the year, but now, apparently, it's resolved. Why hold it against the person, and why bring it up? In fact, employees also remember what happened in the past month or two more readily than events that occurred nine months ago, or see the "distant" past as less relevant. If the intention is to evaluate a full year of performance, this tendency leads to a flawed and inaccurate appraisal.

It is just as inaccurate, by the way, if the employee happens to be having some difficulty at the time the appraisal is completed and you give insufficient emphasis to the early part of the year. Either way you're being overly influenced by a particular moment in time, which may be very misleading. It is certainly not the balanced picture that you want to record.

The only way to counteract this psychological tendency is for the manager to conscientiously record data throughout the year and to base conclusions on what is in the record instead of on how the employee has performed lately. The challenge is to know what is being looked for and to have a disciplined approach to collecting information throughout the year.

Reliance on Gut Feelings

Gut reaction to an employee's performance or behavior is not irrelevant. There's nothing wrong with taking into account a general sense of employees, how able they are and how hard they're trying. By themselves, however, these reactions are notoriously untrustworthy, not legally defensible, and not much use when it comes to giving feedback to the employee. The manager needs to be able to say: "I don't think you're trying hard enough. This is what I mean by trying hard enough. Here's my evidence that in fact you have not met the expectation that we agreed to at the beginning of the year." There must be some evidence to back up a gut reaction; otherwise, employees may argue that you are being subjective and inaccurate. No benefit is likely to come from giving gut reactions even if they are correct; and sometimes—with evidence—you find that the facts modify your gut reaction.

Employee's Miscomprehension of Performance Expectation

Now let's suppose clear standards of performance *have* been established. The manager knows what is expected of the employees but has not explained the standards to the employees. How likely are they to measure up?

If employees aren't given an adequate explanation of the standards by which they're being evaluated, the ratings at the end of the year, even if accurate, may be seen as unfair. Employees may even feel tricked, but most of all, they may not perform well in the first place, because they didn't have a target or benchmark to guide them.

The ideal performance management process takes into account the entire appraisal period. The annual performance appraisal meeting is only one step. A good manager coaches, counsels, monitors, and develops the employees all through the year. It is possible to do that only by making goals and standards clear to the employees and keeping these goals in the forefront of their minds.

In many organizations, the performance appraisal is the only way employees learn what is expected of them. Even if that's not true in your organization, the performance appraisal is your chance to fine-tune that communication.

Employees should know not only what is expected of them, but also, at least in a general way, how judgments are reached. Such an understanding on their part will go a long way toward winning the employees' cooperation in the appraisal process and reducing their defensiveness in the performance appraisal discussion.

Insufficient or Unclear Performance Documentation

It should be obvious that adequate, ongoing documentation is a necessity if a rating manager wants to have more than gut reactions or memory to guide the appraisal. Yet of all the performance appraisal errors, failing to document performance is the most common for two reasons: (1) Managers often experience a shortage of time and energy for a chore that may not seem as important when the performance appraisal is a year away as it will seem when it's just around the corner. In this respect, the performance appraisal is like anything else: Paying attention to details and doing your homework pays off. (2) Managers seem to share a widespread ambivalence about the appraisal process as a whole. Often managers are reluctant to write down anything negative about an employee. Even if they're not hesitant to confront the employee with the problem, they may still think: "Why write it down? Why let it go into the permanent record where it will follow them around for as long as they work here?" To ask these questions is to ask whether performance appraisals should be done at all. Of course they should be done, and they should be done as accurately and thoroughly as possible; but the goal is communication, not paperwork.

We would even argue that documenting performance problems represents a higher form of mercy than keeping them out of the record. An accurate performance record that includes both positive and negative factors will give a better and more balanced picture than the one in which negative factors have been tactfully neglected. It is certainly a necessary basis for a plan that will go to work on this employee's developmental needs.

Also, before giving an individual employee "a break," the manager should consider how it will affect everyone else in the organization. It is not fair to other employees to fail to distinguish between adequate and inadequate performance. Needless to say, if an employee is at last fired for incompetence and the case has to be defended in court, an accurate record will be important. For that matter, suppose the manager at last finds it necessary to take disciplinary action on that individual. If the documentation states that for the past three or four years the employee has been rated "Fully Met Expectations," how will the manager justify that action? The following answer is weak: "Well, I thought I could motivate the employee by giving him a better appraisal than he deserved, but it didn't work." The greater the legal constraints and scrutiny under which a manager operates, the more the documentation has to reflect the actual events.

If an employee is advanced or promoted on the basis of too gentle a performance appraisal, a future manager may one day call the employee's present manager and ask: "What did you do to me?"

Poorly documented appraisals can also hinder employees' advancement. If there is an opportunity elsewhere in the organization, that department manager will look through each candidate's file. If employees' strengths and assets are not presented clearly and accurately, they may not get considered. Now everyone loses. Managers must be sure positive performance is also documented.

Inadequate Time Allotment for the Discussion

It doesn't take long to do a performance appraisal, if you're just going to take the form and read it to the employee. Or hand it to them and say, "Please read this and respond." Some managers like to avoid as much of the appraisal process as possible. This approach reduces interaction and discussion. It is also, undoubtedly, the least useful.

We know of one organization whose regular practice was to have its managers write the appraisal and send it to the employee through interoffice mail with the note, "Please sign and return as soon as possible." Well, that doesn't take much time! However, a manager isn't going to get a lot of behavior change out of that. If the manager's only intention was to give a report card or a grade, then perhaps it would not be unreasonable to do it this way. If, however, the manager wants to use the performance appraisal as a vehicle to develop employees, help them improve in their current job, and perhaps increase their opportunity for advancement or promotion, then he must schedule enough time to discuss the employee's performance in depth. By this, we don't mean merely giving the employee the evaluation, but having a *dialogue* about the implications of the appraisal.

Too Much Talking by Manager/Supervisor

This criticism might seem paradoxical. After all, isn't the point of performance appraisal discussions to let employees know how they have done? They are being given information, right? However, to get the most out of such discussions, managers need to listen as well as talk. They may have completed the appraisal, but there are still things they may need to know. Appraisal discussions provide an opportunity to get at the root of performance problems. To make appraisals motivating for employees, managers need to know what each employee is thinking and feeling and must listen *carefully* to what that employee is saying. Good questioning and listening skills are needed here.

In the employment interview process, an interviewer who does most of the talking is not learning very much; the same thing is true in the performance appraisal process. If, a manager is doing too much talking, he is mainly giving his summary. An employee who is willing to respond may grudgingly agree or accept what the manager says even while being unhappy to hear it. If the manager can get the individual to explain *why* things haven't happened, together they can evolve problem solutions and some kind of plan on which they can agree. Managers need to get their employees involved, and to do that, they have to get the employees to talk more.

Lack of a Follow-Up Plan

If a manager has done everything right, but has no follow up-plan, he is unlikely to succeed. A manager needs to formalize a plan that will improve his employees' performance in their current job, if that's necessary, and then, potentially, improve their capacity to advance and grow. He also needs to talk with employees about how they can keep, support, and advance the mission of the organization over the coming performance period. Having some kind of follow-up plan makes it more likely that that's going to happen.

Structuring the Appraisal Discussion

One of the most common mistakes managers make is to begin the performance appraisal discussion without a clear plan for accomplishing the goals of the meeting. In this chapter, we give you the outline of a structure we suggest Swan Consultants' clients use for the performance appraisal discussion. Clients may not use the exact structure or words we use here, but we can't recommend too strongly that they employ an orderly logical plan or structure that will help them accomplish all their goals during the discussion as well as cover all the subjects they want the discussion to cover.

If you follow our suggestion and conduct an employee self-appraisal session prior to the final performance appraisal discussion, you'll have two meetings with employees: one to discuss their unofficial self-appraisal and one to discuss your official appraisal. If, on the other hand, you *don't* have that initial self-appraisal meeting with employees, you should at least solicit their self-evaluation in writing. Then review their information as one of your sources to make your evaluation accurate. In this instance, you will only have one face-to-face meeting.

You may question whether you need any of the discussion guidelines—it may strike you as odd to see the exact words to say set out on the page. Well, there's no need to use these exact words, or to use this particular plan. But you will need to have some explicit structure if you want to influence the direction and flow of the discussion and keep both you and the employee from going off on tangents, or getting stuck on one point. Using an orderly plan that schedules time for both you and the employee to raise issues that you consider important will reduce the chance that either of you will leave the meeting feeling thwarted. Bear in mind that the structure presented here is just an outline of the discussion, a road map, if you will.

If you meet with employees to discuss their self-evaluation, here are some suggestions.*

* Assumes employees completed a self-evaluation in advance.

Employee Self-Evaluation Discussion

I. Greeting (friendly but brief)

II. Opening Statement

I've been looking forward to this chance to talk with you about your work, and I think this discussion can be helpful for both of us. We'll start by reviewing this past year, and then we'll discuss where we go from here. A good way to start would be for you to review with me your ratings and comments. When we get together for our performance appraisal meeting, I'll give you my perspective, so we can compare. While I'm responsible for the final ratings, I want to give you the opportunity to tell me your point of view.

[Probe with: What . . . Who . . . Tell me . . . How . . . Review . . . Why . . . Explain . . . When . . . Give me an example . . .]

It is important that managers exercise probing and listening skills to get as much high-quality information from their employees as possible, but it's especially important in this meeting because its purpose is specifically to get the employees' input. The employees should do most of the talking, and managers should draw them out, to get their point of view, even with those employees who aren't particularly articulate or who are reticent about explaining themselves.

Otherwise, the general purpose of these first steps should be pretty clear. Like any other meeting on sensitive matters, setting a positive tone with normal social amenities (the greeting) can be important in establishing a relaxed atmosphere, and we provide a suggested opening statement to get the ball rolling.

We don't expect that managers will read this opening statement to the employee; we don't advise them to memorize and recite it. What managers say to begin the discussion is up to them and it will sound more natural if they put it in their own words. But whatever the manager says to the employee to begin the discussion, it should include the points that we've set forth in this sample.

I've been looking forward to this chance to talk with you about your work, and I think this discussion can be helpful for both of us.

Two points are made with this statement that managers may tend to dismiss as soft soap, but they shouldn't be omitted without at least thinking about the purposes they serve:

1. *I've been looking forward to this chance. . . .* Well, maybe the manager has been dreading it! But the manager should be looking forward to the discussion in at least one sense: It's a chance to accomplish something. The discussion isn't just an ordeal that the manager and employee have to get through.

2. *This discussion can be helpful to both of us.* That's exactly right. The discussion is not going to be simply a matter of handing the employee a report card. It's not about delivering the bad news or the good news. It's about what happened this appraisal period, and how that affects what the manager and the employee will be doing during the next appraisal period. It's not about punishment or reward; it's about problem solving, if problems exist.

The second paragraph attempts to minimize any potential defensiveness and establishes the manager's control over the discussion by telling employees exactly what to expect, especially that they will get their chance to respond to the evaluation once it has been explained.

A good way to start would be for you to review with me your ratings and comments. . . .

This assumes that you are meeting to review the employee's self-evaluation, prior to the performance appraisal meeting.

When we get together for our performance appraisal meeting, I'll incorporate your information, and give my perspective, so we can compare.

"My perspective," rather than "then I'll show you where you're wrong," helps establish a tone of reasonableness and sets up some of the discussion that will follow—wherever the manager's evaluation is different from the employee's, the manager is going to need to explain why.

While I'm responsible for the final rating . . .

A manager does not want to deceive the employee: The manager is going to listen to the employee's point of view and use it as one source of input to write the appraisal; the manager will also eventually give the employee a chance to respond to his or her appraisal. But the manager's evaluation is the evaluation of record and this should be made clear at the outset.

. . . I want to give you the opportunity to tell me your point of view, and to ask questions about my ratings and comments.

This sentence makes it clear that the employee will get a chance to make any comments and ask any necessary questions. Letting the employee know that up front makes for a more relaxed, less redundant, less time-consuming, more efficient, more productive discussion.

III. Asking for Employees' Perception of Their Performance

Since you've taken the time to carefully review and complete your copy of the Performance Appraisal Form, let's discuss it. Let's start at the beginning and go through each item one at a time. Let me know what your rating or comment was, and your thinking behind it.

Take notes, do not debate the merits of their statements, listen actively and encourage elaboration.

Again, the form imposes a rational efficient structure on the discussion. Employees will give their point of view, taking "each item one at a time," giving the rating for each item, and justifying that rating. The key point during this part of the discussion is that managers should adhere to the structure as well. Their evaluation of a given item, maybe *every* item, may be strongly at variance with an employee's. Or, the two may agree 100 percent. Whether they agree or disagree, managers should save their point of view for later. They should not debate the merits of their employees' position now, but try to get a clear understanding of their point of view, exactly what it is, and why things look that way to them. A manager's comments and questions should be aimed at reaching that understanding.

Taking notes is advisable precisely because the manager is going to be responding to each item later in the performance appraisal meeting. Listen actively and ask many questions to encourage elaboration. The more clearly you understand not only how the employees rated themselves, but the reasoning behind it, the better you will be able to compare it with your evidence and perceptions when you write the performance appraisal.

IV. Summarizing Their Position

Now let me see if I understand. Your overall assessment of your performance in the past year is . . .

The areas in which you felt you were particularly effective include . . .

Finally, the areas in which you feel you might be able to develop or improve include . . .

Have I summarized accurately?

[Allow for additional clarification if necessary.]

This final statement suggests that managers sum up their employees' self-assessments, so that both parties can check the manager's understanding of what the specific employee has said. As always, the exact words a manager uses aren't important, but it is important to make the key points. The employees' overall assessments should be summed up as accurately as possible. Areas in which they thought they were most effective should be listed; then list the areas in which they thought they could develop or improve. Finally, the employee should be asked if the summary is correct. Occasionally an employee will want to fine-tune the summary to change emphasis or add information; the manager should not rush things; this lets the employee know that getting the full story is important.

Performance Appraisal Discussion

Now, presumably, a week or so have passed since the employee self-appraisal meeting. The manager has reviewed the self-appraisal, has completed the performance appraisal for this employee, and knows where the two versions differ. One advantage of the previous meeting is that it allows the manager to give the appraisal both more diplomatically and more persuasively.

Manager's Evaluation

In our last meeting, we went through your review of yourself, now I'd like to share with you my ratings and comments. I'll start with those areas where we generally agree. Then I'll cover the areas in which our views seem to differ, and give you my reasons for my view.

For Areas of Agreement

- Acknowledge the merits of employee's reactions.
- Add additional information of your own.
- Point out where similar ratings are based on different reasoning if this exists.

For Areas of Disagreement

- Begin with your higher ratings.
- Proceed toward your lowest rating.
- Respond to employee's earlier stated points.
- Give specific examples.
- State your reasons.
- Take extra time and care with sensitive areas.
- End with reference to your overall rating.

The introductory statement, as in the other meeting, structures the meeting in advance by telling what's going to happen.

What was learned from the earlier meeting permits the manager to start with areas of agreement. Some managers might be tempted to do exactly the reverse—save the good news for last and end on an "up" note. In reality, however, beginning with areas of agreement first reduces tension by showing the employee, right away, that there is some common ground and (probably) that all the news is not going to be bad. It is easier to persuade someone when he or she knows that you agree on some things. Furthermore, by going over areas of agreement and telling the employee *why* they agree (which may be different from the employee's reasoning), managers can use these areas of agreement to model their methods for the employee: As a result, the employee will be more easily persuaded when the areas of disagreement are discussed. Employees will be less likely to challenge the fairness or validity of a manager's methods when they've seen the methods work to their benefit.

Presenting areas of agreement first gives managers an opportunity to show employees how judgments were made. This is important because, to the extent possible, managers want to convince their employees of the evaluations' validity. If managers first talk about conclusions that employees don't dispute, they won't be on the defensive and will therefore find it easy to pay attention to the reasoning. The trust that managers build at this point will contribute to the credibility of the presentation a little later, when they move on to the areas of disagreement. That's why, rather than merely saying, "Well, here we're in agreement, let's move on," it's better to give the whole case for each rating. When people agree with us, we're not as prone to examine the logic behind their thinking as we are when they disagree. But if we agree for different reasons, it's important to make that fact clear—we both must understand how we reached our conclusions.

All the other suggestions given under "For Areas of Disagreement" speak to the same purpose of making a convincing case and winning agreement to your point of view. It might take too long to give every incident that contributed to a given conclusion, but managers should give enough specific examples for clarity and to show evidence for the conclusions. Besides stating their reasons, it's important for managers to respond to employees' reasoning for their different self-assessments about that same issue. If a manager disagrees, the employee's reasoning wasn't convincing; but it's not enough to let that just be obvious. To convince the employee, the manager must respond to the arguments and explain why he or she disagrees. And finally, common sense dictates taking extra time and care with sensitive issues. With your final rating, the report card part of the performance appraisal comes to an end.

All these points will help managers be persuasive and will focus the discussion on the desired performance: Not only will employees be persuaded that the ratings are fair, they will come away with a better understanding of the level of performance that is expected for the future.

PART II

DOWNLOADABLE PERFORMANCE APPRAISAL FORMS

CHAPTER 3

A Model Annual Performance Appraisal Form

One could argue that a performance appraisal form is only a vehicle to record the manager's implementation of an organization's performance management system. We have often told the managers who attend our *How to Do a Superior Performance Appraisal* training program that the form is only meant to support the ongoing performance management process; and if the managers knew, understood, and used their system effectively, they could summarize their employees' performance on a blank sheet of paper. As a practical matter, however, the closer the form is to that system, the more likely it will be that an individual manager will follow the system, and across many managers, the process becomes more consistent. It also makes the tasks of managers easier, since the template of a good form allows them to concentrate on content. The question now becomes what should be included on a good performance appraisal form.

This chapter introduces the performance appraisal form we recommend to our clients; to be more precise, it's an ideal or model version of that form, which can be easily adapted to the particular circumstances of any organization. It is based on the observation that performance for any job has two components: how the employees behaved against standards or expectations, usually called the *competencies*, and what the employees accomplished against the objectives or goals they were assigned. No performance appraisal system or form can give a balanced picture of performance unless it addresses both these aspects of the job.

Competencies refer to how employees do their job on an ongoing basis. They often represent an organization's core values or expectations, and by placing them on the form, management increases the likelihood that every manager is discussing and setting standards for direct reports on these dimensions. Said another way, while the exact behavior we expect for the competency of "Provides Good and Timely Customer Service" may vary depending on the job, management wants to be sure that every manager sets standards for every employee on that core competency. Thus, the form lists the same set of competencies for all employees. Some forms add specific management competencies for employees who are in a managerial position.

Chapter 6 presents twenty-one core competencies most commonly used in business today, plus four managerial competencies.

Objectives or goals, unlike competencies, are unique to an individual, and are usually different from one appraisal period to the next. It is quite possible that several employees with the same job title or role, would be responsible for different objectives or goals during a given appraisal period. This represents the manager's allocation of different projects, tasks, or assignments that need to be accomplished across several employees. Individual performance objectives are assigned at the beginning of each appraisal period and may be added to or modified during that period. They focus employee efforts to help implement this year's organizational, department, or unit performance objectives. A good performance appraisal form will provide an opportunity not only to evaluate last year's results against objectives, but also prompts both the manager and employee to set new objectives for the coming year.

As shown in the summary that follows and on the Model Annual Performance Appraisal Form provided at the end of this chapter (Form 3.1), this form supports a two-part process. First, there's the Report Card Phase (Part I, Part II, and Part III of the form). During this phase, managers give employees feedback on their performance with reference to their performance objectives (focused activities) and the competencies (the ongoing job requirements or behaviors) set at the beginning of the year. In Part III, an integrated summary of total performance is documented. This Report Card Phase measures the past, and is where most performance appraisal forms stop. The method set forth in this chapter goes beyond that point, however. There is a second phase, which concerns the future (Parts IV and V of the form).

Part IV, the Development Plan, is where a manager documents a plan for improving employee performance by setting an agreed-on series of tasks. The goal of the Development Plan is to move the individual forward (unlike performance objectives, which are intended to move the organization forward). It can be used to bring employees up to standard, to prepare them for advancement, or to provide job enrichment experiences for highly successful employees.

On Part V of the form, the manager and the employee work out next year's performance plan by establishing and agreeing on the performance objectives. While it might be inevitable that new assignments will be added during the year (which become part of the next end-of-the-year review), there is a unique opportunity in the performance appraisal session to tie in individual objectives with the organizational or departmental goals or objectives for that year.

It might be helpful for the reader to track the following summary of the components of the Model Annual Performance Appraisal Form against the actual form provided at the end of this chapter. And remember that this form is available to you as a downloadable document.

Phase 1 (the Report Card)

I. Objectives
    How successful was the employee at meeting special goals agreed to at the beginning of the Appraisal Period (as modified or adjusted during that period)?

II. Performance Factors (Competencies)
    How well did the employee perform during the appraisal period as measured against standards or competencies reflecting identified organization-wide core values and the needs of this role.

III. Overall Evaluation for This Appraisal Period
    This is a summary evaluation based on Part I and Part II.

Phase 2 (Planning for the Future)

IV. The Development Plan

    A. This section should include a specific plan for improving employees' effectiveness in their current job. It should include areas identified as needing strengthening in the "report card" phase.

B. This is a plan to provide preparatory experiences for advancement or promotion, so the employee is ready if and when opportunities open up.

C. Alternatively (if advancement is not likely or not of interest to the successful employee), a plan can be created to enrich the employee's experience of the everyday job.

V. Performance Plan

New performance objectives are set for the next appraisal period. These performance objectives move the organization or department forward and are linked with organization/department goals and objectives. These objectives become the objectives listed on Part I of the form at the next performance appraisal. If they are modified or adjusted during the year, the final modified version becomes the objectives listed in Part I.

These, then, are the basic elements I recommend for a performance management form. But performance management is a *process*, not a form or a grab bag of appraisal techniques. To appreciate the usefulness of this approach, you have to see how these elements are played off each other throughout the appraisal period and beyond it.

Eight Steps of Performance Management

Performance management is not a single event. It continues throughout the appraisal period. When the appraisal period is over, performance management doesn't come to an end; it continues in a cycle. Step 8 of this year's appraisal period happens at the same meeting as Step 1 of the next year's appraisal:

1. Manager and employee agree to performance plan and development plan.

2. Ongoing feedback, coaching, counseling, and documentation are maintained for the next year.

3. As time of appraisal approaches and prior to writing the performance appraisal, manager solicits employee's self-evaluation.

4. Manager meets with the employee to discuss employee's self-evaluation (or at least reviews the employee's written self-evaluation).

5. Manager completes the Report Card portion (Parts I through III) of the performance appraisal form.

6. Manager previews appraisal with his or her manager or human resources (some organizations require this step. If your company does not, consider doing it anyway for more difficult appraisal situations).

7. Manager schedules appraisal meeting with employee.

8. Manager conducts appraisal discussion.

MODEL ANNUAL PERFORMANCE APPRAISAL FORM*
Downloadable Form 3.1

Name: _____   Date_____

Part I: Review of Progress toward Meeting Last Year's Objectives

Objectives/Projects	Results	Weighting	Rating
(As modified during the year)	(Narrative)	(Must total 100%)	

1.

           Greatly exceeded expectation ❑
Consistently exceeded expectation ❑
————— Fully met expectation ❑
Did not meet expectation ❑
Significantly below expectation ❑

2.

           Greatly exceeded expectation ❑
Consistently exceeded expectation ❑
————— Fully met expectation ❑
Did not meet expectation ❑
Significantly below expectation ❑

3.

           Greatly exceeded expectation ❑
Consistently exceeded expectation ❑
————— Fully met expectation ❑
Did not meet expectation ❑
Significantly below expectation ❑

4.

           Greatly exceeded expectation ❑
Consistently exceeded expectation ❑
————— Fully met expectation ❑
Did not meet expectation ❑
Significantly below expectation ❑

5.

           Greatly exceeded expectation ❑
Consistently exceeded expectation ❑
————— Fully met expectation ❑
Did not meet expectation ❑
Significantly below expectation ❑

Overall Weighted Average Rating for Objectives _____

MODEL ANNUAL PERFORMANCE APPRAISAL FORM
Downloadable Form 3.1 *(Continued)*

Part II: Review of Progress toward Meeting Expectations of Performance Agreed to Last Year

Perfomance Factors (Examples)	Weighting (Must total 100%)	Rating	
1. Customer Service		Greatly exceeded expectation	❏
		Consistently exceeded expectation	❏
	————	Fully met expectation	❏
		Did not meet expectation	❏
		Significantly below expectation	❏
2. Quality of Work		Greatly exceeded expectation	❏
		Consistently exceeded expectation	❏
	————	Fully met expectation	❏
		Did not meet expectation	❏
		Significantly below expectation	❏
3. Quantity of Work		Greatly exceeded expectation	❏
		Consistently exceeded expectation	❏
	————	Fully met expectation	❏
		Did not meet expectation	❏
		Significantly below expectation	❏
4. Teamwork/Cooperation		Greatly exceeded expectation	❏
		Consistently exceeded expectation	❏
	————	Fully met expectation	❏
		Did not meet expectation	❏
		Significantly below expectation	❏
5. Initiative/Motivation		Greatly exceeded expectation	❏
		Consistently exceeded expectation	❏
	————	Fully met expectation	❏
		Did not meet expectation	❏
		Significantly below expectation	❏
6. Communication Skills		Greatly exceeded expectation	❏
		Consistently exceeded expectation	❏
	————	Fully met expectation	❏
		Did not meet expectation	❏
		Significantly below expectation	❏

(continued)

MODEL ANNUAL PERFORMANCE APPRAISAL FORM
Downloadable Form 3.1 *(Continued)*

Perfomance Factors (Examples)	Weighting (Must total 100%)	Rating	
7. Technical Skills/Comman of Knowledge		Greatly exceeded expectation	❏
		Consistently exceeded expectation	❏
	————	Fully met expectation	❏
		Did not meet expectation	❏
		Significantly below expectation	❏
8. Management/Leadership		Greatly exceeded expectation	❏
		Consistently exceeded expectation	❏
	————	Fully met expectation	❏
		Did not meet expectation	❏
		Significantly below expectation	❏
9. Efficient Internal Operations		Greatly exceeded expectation	❏
		Consistently exceeded expectation	❏
	————	Fully met expectation	❏
		Did not meet expectation	❏
		Significantly below expectation	❏

Overall Weighted Average Rating for Objectives _____

Part III: Summary of Overall Performance for Year

Weighted Average of Objectives and Performance Factors

Greatly exceeded expectation of performance	❏
Consistently exceeded expectation	❏
Fully met expectation	❏
Did not meet expectation	❏
Significantly below expectation of performance	❏

Narrative summary:

_____

_____

_____

_____

_____

_____

_____

MODEL ANNUAL PERFORMANCE APPRAISAL FORM
Downloadable Form 3.1 *(Continued)*

Part IV: Development Plan

A. For use if any individual rating is below "fully met expectation," or if employee wants to work on an area of current job.

For improvement in current job, the following actions/objectives have been agreed to:

1. _____
2. _____
3. _____

B. For use if advancement or career growth is a practical option and employee is interested.

For preparation for possible advancement, the following actions/objectives have been agreed to:

1. _____
2. _____
3. _____

C. Job enrichment: For use if advancement or career growth is not an option, or if employee is not interested.

The following actions/objectives have been agreed to:

1. _____
2. _____
3. _____

Part V: Perfomance Plan

These are the objectives or projects that employee and manager agree on for the next year (additions or modifications are to be done in writing). *These objectives become the subject matter of Part I of the form for next year.*

1. _____
2. _____
3. _____
4. _____
5. _____
6. _____

(continued)

MODEL ANNUAL PERFORMANCE APPRAISAL FORM
Downloadable Form 3.1 *(Continued)*

Part VI: Employee Statement

(Optional—Additional sheets may be used)

_____

_____

_____

_____

_____

Part VII: Signatures

_____   _____

Manager (Direct Supervisor)   Date   Employee   Date

(Signature acknowledges that this form has been
reviewed with employee. It does not imply
agreement with content).

Initials   Initials
Prior to   Prior to
Appraisal   Appraisal
Discussion (   )   Discussion (   )

Department Manager   Date   Human Resources   Date

CHAPTER 4

Implementing the Model Annual Performance Appraisal Form

When deciding on competencies, creating a rating scale, or dealing with your existing form, *competencies* and *behaviors* are commonly used terms in performance management. They are subsets of the concept of *performance factors,* which is the term we will use in this chapter. Performance factors might be broadly defined as *how* employees do their jobs, in contrast to the other component of full performance, *performance objectives.* Objectives represent *what* a person accomplishes (projects, assignments, tasks). Taken together, Objectives and Performance factors represent the totality of ongoing job performance. They are found in Parts I and II of the Model Annual Performance Appraisal Form, and are integrated in Part III. Since objectives are usually individualized for each person, in the following discussion, we focus on performance factors. They probably are already in existence on your organization's performance appraisal form and are to be used for all employees. Chapter 6 provides downloadable, detailed narrative summaries for the most common performance factors.

It might seem obvious that as a manager, I'd be well pleased if my employees were to successfully introduce a new product on time and within the preset cost constraints. Suppose, however, that in meeting those objectives, they alienated key members of another department, making it less likely that I'll have that department's cooperation in the future. Then I wouldn't be as pleased. An organization can't help but be concerned with *how* a job gets done, and this aspect of job performance is best measured by performance factors. It is a major component of Form 3.1 and deserves a more complete treatment here. Therefore, all the 25 competencies introduced in Chapter 6, along with the downloadable set of evaluative statements, are performance factors.

Performance Factors

The following list outlines the four values of performance factors:

1. *Provide managers and employees with consistent definition of quality performance.* What kind of on-the-job behavior goes into doing the job *right?* What are the ingredients? The performance factors not only set a standard to be used to evaluate the employees, but also show employees what to shoot for.

2. *Reinforce the core values of the organization.* Performance factors are generally chosen at the policy-setting level of the organization. They're meant to embody the values the organization considers important. The performance factors can be an organization's way of saying: "These are the values that we want our employees to actualize and through which we want them to represent us; this is what we stand for." It puts the mission statement into action.

3. *Provide coaching tools for improving future performance.* How employees are performing their jobs is precisely what a manager must monitor to coach and counsel the employees effectively. If employees are not meeting their performance objectives, there's a good chance that a glance at the way they stack up on the performance factors will show what they're doing wrong and why they're not meeting their objectives.

4. *Support individual effectiveness and overall organizational performance.* Performance factors are chosen because they work. We know from experience or from analysis of the job that they're important standards of behavior. While performance objectives measure the contribution that a specific employee was responsible for, performance factors encourage behaviors that are known to be beneficial in the long run, even when management can't document their link to an immediate positive outcome. There is no doubt that if every employee were to provide truly excellent customer service, it would be a positive benefit for the organization.

Sources of Performance Factors

In some shape or other, by some name or other, most performance appraisal forms have a component similar to this "laundry list" of qualities that I am referring to as performance factors. It is the most widely used performance appraisal approach.

Ideally, performance factors have been carefully selected by an organization to reflect those issues or values that it sees as important. They are job relevant and relevant to the goals of the organization. Some organizations even include performance factors like "contribution to profitability" or "commitment to affirmative action plan." As a rule, they're set on an organization-wide basis, usually for all employees in a category (the categories are typically "exempt" and "nonexempt," but sometimes include "professional/technical" and "manager/supervisor"). Occasionally, there are separate or additional performance factors for technical professionals and managers.

While as a rule, a manager will establish individual performance objectives in cooperation with each employee at the beginning of the appraisal period, it is not likely that the individual manager will have the responsibility of choosing the performance factors (although the manager will set the standard of performance and weighting for each of them). But if you have any input into the decisions that go into drawing up or altering your organization's list of performance factors, here are some tips on where to find performance factors that are specific, job relevant, and measurable.

Because performance factors are generally desirable permanent characteristics of an employee, managers can arrive at them by analyzing the job requirements the same way they would analyze them when preparing to hire new employees. In fact, those of you who have read Dr. Swan's book, *Swan's How to Pick the Right People Program* (New York: John Wiley & Sons, 1989), or have been through Swan Consultants' "How to Pick the Right People" selection interview workshop will recognize the three categories we're about to discuss. They're useful for determining job requirements when you're preparing to interview a job candidate. They're just as useful as a source of performance factors. They represent the totality of any job in a way that transcends the more obvious factors, which are usually covered by a job description.

Knowledge, Skills, and Abilities

The first category represents what human resource professionals call the "KSAs": the "knowledge, skills, and abilities" necessary for success. Exactly what knowledge base, what presentation skills, what verbal or analytical skills are necessary? What level of technical knowledge, territory management exposure, or product knowledge do incumbents need for this job? What do they have to know to be successful and—because in the context of the performance appraisal this is an ongoing process—are they keeping their knowledge current?

Knowledge, skills, and abilities thus represent an arena from which one might select the job requirements that will become performance factors. These are the things managers first think of when they think of an individual's competence, and they're the performance factors that are the most specific to an individual job—the least likely to apply to all the organization's employees. As performance factors, the KSAs are useful in pinpointing easy-to-repair deficits in performance. If "effective presentation skills" is a performance factor and a manager discovers that an employee has a weakness in this area, that diagnosis can be an effective springboard for a developmental plan.

Behaviors

The second arena includes qualities that are subtle and harder to define and that are often thought of as personality traits: things such as initiative, motivation, drive for success, and reliability. Think of them as behaviors, not traits, to underline that, for the performance appraisal and selection interview, they should be defined in a way that makes them measurable. How would an employee have to behave to *show* the initiative or the drive for success needed on this job?

Managers often have wildly different definitions of these words. That doesn't mean, however, that they don't describe realities that are important for high-quality job performance. But for these words to be useful, there must be general agreement among managers on what the words mean in relation to a given job—and that the message must be communicated to the employee.

As a manager, what do I mean by initiative: Do I want my employees to show some degree of independence (e.g., when I suggest an idea, they give me their points of view)? That's not the same as the initiative they might display by launching a project of their own without asking. Perhaps some managers would applaud one kind of initiative but wouldn't want to encourage the other. These managers should be sure to define the term, both for themselves and for the employee.

An organization might feel that "a positive response to direction and authority" is vital for employees at a certain level. By this, it may mean that after the employees have given their opinions or inputs, and once the manager has decided how to proceed, employees then execute the plan with their full effort and without further argument. Organizations don't want a "yes" person, but they don't want someone who will debate with management forever.

Environmental Factors

The third arena or aspect of any job is the environment in which employees have to work. Often this includes facts that management is reluctant to acknowledge, but that are tacitly known by everyone who works at an organization or in a particular division or department. If the ability and willingness to cope with these realities is necessary for high quality and productivity, this requirement should be noted when you're drawing up the performance factors. Do employees have to deal with deadline pressure? Do they have to show political savvy and tact when coping with arbitrariness and capriciousness? Ethics and confidentiality may have been recently reinforced as important values. If so, that intention can and should be spelled out in the performance factors.

It is unlikely that a hundred skills, behaviors, or environmental factors are important enough to the job or to the organization to be made into standard performance factors. Chances are that two or three from each category will serve, yielding 8 to 12 performance factors.

In an ideal performance management program, there would probably be a core group of performance factors that express values important to the organization as a whole, and that would therefore be part of the performance appraisal for every job: others, especially skills, but also some performance factors drawn from job-relevant behaviors and environmental factors, would be different for each job or job family.

In Chapter 6 we have provided detailed evaluation statements for 21 core competencies and 4 managerial performance factors (competencies). You can download and customize these statements to help you complete your performance appraisal forms. If you are developing a new performance appraisal form for your organization, you can select from these competencies those that work best for you.

Note that these competencies are drawn for all three categories discussed earlier. For example, Communication is a "Skill or Ability" item,

Initiative is a "Behavior" and Ethics and Standards are "Environmental" issues.

How to Decide on a Rating Scale

While performance objectives are usually either met or not, performance factors aren't cut and dried. Therefore, any performance factors arrived at must include some way of recording gradations of performance. In effective performance appraisals, we just can't escape making an evaluative judgment. It is a process we have grown accustomed to from school where we were introduced to the scale A, B, C, D, F. Most people continue, in every area of life, to be evaluated according to some sort of scale; and with remarkable regularity, it turns out to be a 5-point scale (the ABCDF of our early schooling was a 5-point scale).

There are actually sound reasons for this. Whenever clients insist on using a 3-point scale (say, outstanding, satisfactory, unsatisfactory), they soon realize that it almost immediately becomes a 5-point scale anyway. Somehow, raters cannot resist putting notches between the three points. Too many employees turn out to be a little better than "satisfactory" but not quite "outstanding," a little less than "satisfactory" but not quite "unsatisfactory." Because 3-point scales become 5-point scales anyway, we might as well start them out that way.

On the other hand, a scale of more than 5 points makes an implicit claim to precision that is hard to justify unless relying solely on easily quantifiable objective evidence such as sales figures or numbers of widgits produced per hour: It is not generally possible for the evaluation of performance factors (competencies or behaviors). Finally, a 5-point scale is perceived by most people as reasonable. While the top and bottom points on the scale are rarely used for the overall rating of performance (Part III of Form 3.1), on an individual objective or competency, they might be an accurate indication of the employee's performance.

It is important to note that the midpoint of the scale ("3," Fully Met Expectation) is not average, lackluster performance. It is not the "C" Grade we are familiar with from school. Instead, if you must have a grade analogy, it is more like a "B." This means that when we set a standard or expectation it requires real effort, the result is meaningful, and the person is rated as "Fully Met Expectation" on that item. Employees are compensated for doing an effective job, not just showing up. Therefore, we set reasonable and strong expectations for them. The average or lackluster performance mentioned earlier would be rated "2," "Did Not Meet Expectation." This approach has successfully controlled grade inflation and skewed rating in many organizations. However it does require that employees be told in advance of the expectations set. Also, success (meaning performing at the Fully Met Expectation level) is rewarded through reasonable recognition (merit increases, promotional opportunities, and expressed appreciation).

On Form 3.1, the ratings are not associated with letters or numbers. The scale for performance factors may translate into numbers as managers eventually reach for an overall rating on an employee. But for purposes of discussion between the manager and the employee, it's better to avoid numbers or letters. The manager doesn't want to reduce the employee to a number. He or she doesn't want to encourage the employee to think of it as a grade, but to focus on performance. The words are better. They shift attention from the grade to its meaning. Instead of saying "Maria, on this competency I rated you a 3," it would be better to say "Maria, on this competency you fully met the expectation we agreed on, and thanks."

The use of the scale makes it necessary for managers to know what level of performance is associated with each numeric point. So not only do the managers have to know what they mean (and what the organization means) by the term *initiative;* but they ought to know what an employee must do to meet or exceed the expectation set, and what behaviors would fall short of it.

A definition of initiative might go like this: "Well, I expect that when you come to me with a problem, you think it through in advance and present a solution or options. If, as a routine procedure throughout the year when you come to me with a problem, you have thought it through and have given me two or three reasonable options, one of which you recommend, then I would rate you as 'met the expectation' for initiative. If you solve most problems effectively before you come to me, that would merit the rating of 'consistently exceeded expectation.' If you often bring me problems without possible solutions or with solutions that aren't workable or realistic, I would have to rate you as 'did not meet expectation' for this competency."

By the way, managers should think carefully about the distance between the midpoint of the scale, which is the anchor point, and other points on the scale. There's a temptation to see the list as representing a scale ascending and descending in equal increments, but this may not reflect the reality of the job. If having met the standard means the employee should get at least 10 of the 12 monthly reports in on the due date and two no more than one week late, that would be the standard. However, "consistently exceeded expectation" isn't necessarily earned by an occasional foray into high-level behavior. That is why we recommend the use of the word *consistently*. Over the course of the year, what is the pattern of behavior? An occasional but not consistent elevated level of performance does not merit a higher rating, but the manager would recognize it in the narrative statement for that competency.

If you've ever taken a course in negotiation skills, you may be familiar with this kind of thinking. Suppose someone says to you, "I'll offer you $420,000 for your house," and you say, "No, I want $450,000"; and the potential buyer says, "Okay, I'd like to make this deal work, I'll offer you $430,000." Well, your next bid need not be $440,000—it could be $449,000. Just because the party you're negotiating with went up $10,000 doesn't mean you have to go down the same amount. Yet that's what people often do out of a love of symmetry.

The same logic applies to the standards used for the performance factors. They should be fair, they should reflect the realities of the job, and they should be consistent from employee to employee; but they needn't be symmetrical. In fact, it is more likely that a geometric relationship exists for the different levels of performance.

As a further suggestion regarding rating employees, be mindful that highly effective employees report that their managers sometimes concentrate their time on problem employees and they do not get recognition or appreciation for their efforts. For example, high-level performers value reading and hearing specific examples of how their performance has exceeded expectations. If we take this group for granted and do not give them detailed feedback on their successful performance, we risk lowering motivation and commitment on their part. Remember that our job as managers is not only to correct performance where needed but to sustain high levels of achievement where it exists.

On the other end of the performance continuum, you should not be hesitant to use the lowest rating on the rating scale, if the employee's performance on an individual objective or performance factor was far off the mark from what was expected. We did say earlier that for the overall rating for the year it is not common that the very highest or lowest points on a five-point scale will be used (that would require perfection or complete failure on every dimension of performance). But for any individual item being evaluated, it is possible that the lowest rating applies. You are not doing the employee a service by allowing her to believe that she was just a little short of the mark when that is not correct. You should also offer to provide (and through the Development Plan formalize) assistance and support to help her achieve a higher rating next time.

What If Your Organization's Form Is Different from the Model Annual Performance Appraisal Form?

The model shown as Form 3.1 supports the best balance of elements to ensure a fair and accurate performance appraisal. It puts the performance appraisal to its best use and wins cooperation and commitment from employees. We recommend that you apply this process if you can.

But what if you aren't free to do whatever you want? Most managers are asked to implement a performance appraisal form they receive as a fait accompli. How can you apply the lessons presented so far? Can you use your organization's form and, at the same time, conduct a performance management process that gives you the benefits we've described?

In most cases, you can. The performance appraisal systems of most organizations are either similar to Form 3.1 (perhaps giving different names to the various elements) or contain one element among the several presented here. Usually, the manager has a great deal of latitude in applying the performance appraisal. One might say, the more inadequate and haphazard the form, the more latitude you have in using it.

If your organization's performance appraisal system is inadequate to the tasks it must perform, you may have room to take action to repair the faults in the system. Where the criteria for the appraisal are lax, vague, or insufficiently job related, you can use those labels, but define them for your employees in a concrete, job-related way. When a formal component of the Model Annual Performance Appraisal Form is missing, you can supplement your form. For example, if you think Part IV of Form 3.1 (the Development Plan) is useful, but it's not on your organization's form, there is no reason you cannot use it. In fact, attaching additional documentation to a performance appraisal form is rarely a problem.

What if Your Organization's System Only Covers Performance Factors?

In some organizations, the performance appraisal form consists entirely of a list of traits or behaviors for which top management supplies no definition or standard. To shape this performance appraisal into a more useful one for your purposes, you might use two basic strategies:

1. Define the traits in a more job-relevant fashion.
2. Give your employees performance objectives and evaluate them on how well they achieve them.

Define the Traits in a More Concrete Fashion

Energy, motivation, initiative, cooperation—what's wrong with a manager wanting employees to have these qualities? Nothing, providing the manager can define them in a concrete job-relevant way.

To be defendable as fair performance appraisal criteria and to lead to better performance instead of pointless misunderstandings, traits and behaviors should be given specific definitions. That way, employees will know what is really being said and what they need to do to meet the standard.

To be useful, these definitions should relate as specifically as possible to the actual requirements of the particular job—every employee in the organization may be expected to show initiative if that is a value your organization prizes, but what we expect for initiative is going to mean one thing for a vice president and another for an customer service representative. So while keeping faith with your organization's identification of initiative, you should tell your direct reports what you are expecting of them on the competency of initiative.

Your organization may not have any guidelines closely defining the traits in its list of personal qualities or behaviors expected of employees, but that doesn't prevent you from having a concrete definition of your own for each trait. All it requires is a little research and a little thinking, relating each trait to the job in question. Ask people who know something about the job—your employees, managers who supervise that position, people who interface with that job—and ask yourself what is meant by each term with respect to that particular position.

In addition to defining the qualities more concretely, you should first review the list to make sure that it includes all the qualities for which you want to hold your organization responsible. You may want to add to that list. Those additional items may or may not become an official part of the performance appraisal, depending on your organization's policies and how much latitude you are given.

What If Your Organization's System Includes Objectives but Not Performance Factors?

The performance appraisal form of some organizations consists of a piece of paper that says "Objectives" over one column and "Results" over another. If you have a system that includes objectives but not performance factors, you will recognize that it's one thing for a manager to evaluate employees on whether they met their objective, but *how* they met their objective is still an important issue. That is an issue performance factors were meant to address.

Suppose the employees met objective number three, but they did it in a way that alienated individuals in another department and jeopardized gaining cooperation for future projects? The employees need to get feedback, and the manager has a right to let them know that how they achieve their objectives is important and will be included in the evaluation. Otherwise, next year they could say, "Well I met my objective again; you never said you were evaluating how I did it." Therefore, on that "Results" column the manager *should* indicate any qualifying issues about how those objectives were met.

It is not critical that you have a part of the form called "Performance Factors" and another part called "Performance Objectives." The important thing is to make sure that your appraisals reflect both components of the job.

What If Your Organization Uses the Global Essay System?

If your organization uses the *global essay* form of the performance appraisal, then, almost by definition anything goes—the manager has complete latitude to apply every suggestion in this book. A global essay approach by definition leaves everything up to the manager: to assign employees performance factors and performance objectives at the beginning of the year, to explain how they work, to monitor and coach during the year on these issues, and so on. The manager can even make it official by explaining the process in the essay section: Such a global essay will be fair, rational, and defendable.

When Your Performance Appraisal Program Changes Course

Here is an interesting question that comes up in Swan Consultants' seminars occasionally: "Okay, suppose we take your advice—starting this year we set performance objectives, define standards of performance on the performance factors, and base the performance appraisal on data we collect throughout the year. There's bound to be a sudden change in many of our employees' ratings based on this change in our procedures. How do we deal with that?"

Well, to take this objection to its logical conclusion, what's the alternative? Would you continue to rate employees inaccurately so as not to create a discrepancy between this year's rating and last year's? Of course not. At some point, it is necessary to wake up and say: "I haven't been as organized and clear as I could have these past couple years regarding the performance appraisal process, but here's how we're going to proceed this coming year."

All managers can do is be clear and candid, and give employees fair warning of the new approach. This year, when they sit down with their employees, it's the beginning a new cycle. The manager would say, "It's clear to me that last year I never really clarified for you what I really expected. This year will be different. Together, we're going to develop the plan for next year, and I'm going to make clear what I'm expecting of you. I can tell you exactly what you need to do for you to get an overall rating that meets the expectation or exceeds it."

If the employees are sharp, they will recognize that the game plan has changed and they're going to be held more accountable for their actions than they have been before. It's like getting a new English teacher who says at the beginning of the year: "You're going to have three book reports, and if they're not in by the date they're due, you automatically drop by one letter grade." And they will think, "I did pretty well in my previous English class without working very hard, but I can see that this class is going to require more attention on my part."

If you are asked how an employee who has been rated "Exceptional" for the past three years could be now rated "Fully Met Expectation," the answer is that you and the employee agreed on clear standards of performance, and for the year the employee has performed at the level of "Fully Met Expectation." If there is a difference in this year's ratings, it is because there is a more rigorous process in place.

CHAPTER 5

Sample Forms from Different Companies

In this chapter, we have assembled several real-world performance appraisal forms. Each one has been selected for some particular uniqueness of design, layout, or application. While we have eliminated company-specific identifiers and made modifications, the unique features we want to share with you have been preserved. We are not necessarily recommending these forms, but are presenting them for your review and to let you see how other organizations are approaching the performance management process. For a form we do recommend, see Form 3.1 in Chapter 3 (downloadable).

We present some of the forms in their entirety; whereas for others, we have selected only the page or pages that display their uniqueness. Supplementary information on the forms such as legal disclaimers, development plans, and/or signature boxes have not been included.

The forms presented are used by managers for their year-end reviews. Self-evaluations, when incorporated as part of the form, are shown, but otherwise, forms for additional party feedback (e.g., self, peers, clients, stakeholders) have not been included.

Downloadable Form 5.1 includes the following unique characteristics:

- A 5-point rating scale, used for the Overall Rating, Employee Goals, Core Competencies, and Supervisory/Leadership Responsibilities.

- Presentation of the Overall Rating as the first rating viewed on the form; a thorough description of the rating scale including a specific description of each of the five performance levels.

- Use of letters for the rating scale terms for ratings (e.g., D [distinguished], EP [excellent performer]).

- Employee's self-ratings and supervisor ratings included on the same form.

- A section on Employee Goals, with space to include the goals, status, or accomplishments and a rating on each; six Core Competencies and three Supervisory/Leadership Responsibilities for evaluation.

- Employees are rated on specific items under each competency and not on the overall competency. All employees are rated on the same competencies (supervisory, only if applicable).

- There is space for supervisor comments after the Employee Goals section as well as after each competency. These comments take the place of any overall comments. Comments are required if the highest or lowest ends of the rating scale are used.

COMPANY SAMPLE FORM #1*
Downloadable Form 5.1

Performance Evaluation

Employee's Name:	Department:
Employee's Title:	Supervisor's Name:
Hire Date:	Supervisor's Title:

Overall Rating   *(Please circle)*

D	EP	ME	NI	U
Distinguished	Excellent Performer	Meets Expectations	Needs Improvement	Unsatisfactory

Rating Scale

These employees *consistently* exceed the expectations of their position. Their management and colleagues recognize their excellence and their unique contributions. They serve as a role model for the organization. They would be considered a top performer in any high-performing organization. Only a small percentage of employees fall in this category.	Distinguished D
These employees *frequently* exceed and provide significant and measurable contributions *well beyond their position responsibilities*. These employees would be considered above average in any top-performing organization.	Excellent Performer EP
These employees *meet the basic expectations for the position.* In some instances, this rating is appropriate for those new to a position. In other instances, this may reflect mixed performance: employees who do some things well but who need to strengthen other areas of their performance. The majority of employees should fall into this category.	Meets Expectations ME
These employees *require improvement* in quality, quantity and/or timeliness of their work. Their performance may have been successful on some occasions, but it *frequently* fell below expectations. These employees are below average at their current level of performance.	Needs Improvement NI
These employees *are not meeting the expectations of their position.* They should be on a formal Performance Improvement Plan. This level suggests either a lack of willingness and/or ability to perform the requirements of their position. Separation may be indicated unless the employee's performance improves significantly and the improvement is sustained.	Unsatisfactory U

---

*To customize this document, download to your hard drive from www.wiley.com/go/PerformanceAppraisalForms. The document can then be opened, edited, and printed for personal use only, using Microsoft Word or another popular word processing application.

(continued)

COMPANY SAMPLE FORM #1
Downloadable Form 5.1 *(Continued)*

Part I: Employee Goals

Goals are special tasks, new skills, unique projects, or assignments that go above and beyond day-to-day responsibilities.

Rating Scale				
D	EP	ME	NI	U
Distinguished	Excellent Performer	Meets Expectations	Needs Improvement	Unsatisfactory
	Prior Year's Goals	Status/Accomplishments	Employee Rating	Supervisor Rating
A				
B				
C				
D				
E				
Supervisor's Comments:				

COMPANY SAMPLE FORM #1
Downloadable Form 5.1 *(Continued)*

Part II: Core Competencies

Questions in this section require comments if the rating is a D or U

1. Approach to Work The employee demonstrates:	Employee Self-Rating	Supervisor Rating
self-motivation		
flexibility and adaptability		
enthusiasm		
pride in his/her accomplishments		
Supervisor's Comments:		

2. Professional Attitude The employee:	Employee Self-Rating	Supervisor Rating
works effectively under pressure		
exhibits a positive attitude		
treats coworkers and other associates with professionalism and respect		
welcomes, responds, and takes corrective actions to constructive criticism		
Supervisor's Comments:		

3. Job Knowledge The employee:	Employee Self-Rating	Supervisor Rating
commands base knowledge to perform the job		
knows and demonstrates their basic job responsibilities		
consistently attempts to expand their job knowledge and keeps abreast of new developments in their field		
Supervisor's Comments:		

4. Interpersonal/Communication Skills The employee:	Employee Self-Rating	Supervisor Rating
communicates effectively with all levels both orally and in writing		
has the confidence of other people		
shares information appropriately, timely, with tact and diplomacy		
keeps his/her supervisors informed as appropriate		
Supervisor's Comments:		

(continued)

COMPANY SAMPLE FORM #1
Downloadable Form 5.1 *(Continued)*

5. Judgment/Decision-Making Skills The employee:	Employee Self-Rating	Supervisor Rating
sets and carries out priorities		
balances competing and/or conflicting interests		
develops logical and creative solutions to problems and makes effective decisions		
Supervisor's Comments		

6. Time Management The employee:	Employee Self-Rating	Supervisor Rating
adheres to departmental attendance and punctuality guidelines	Y/N	Y/N
schedules effectively and makes efficient use of time while at work	Y/N	Y/N
Supervisor's Comments:		

Part III: Supervisory/Leadership Responsibilities

Rating Scale				
D	EP	ME	NI	U
Distinguished	Excellent Performer	Meets Expectations	Needs Improvement	Unsatisfactory

Questions in this section require comments if the rating is a D or U.

1. Supervisory Responsibility The employee:	Employee Self-Rating	Supervisor Rating
trains, develops, and mentors his/her staff		
faces performance issues candidly and squarely		
clearly sets achievable goals for department		
ensures that goals are met on a timely and accurate basis		
ensures that he/she and his/her staff comply with training requirements		
develops, delivers timely and meaningful Performance Evaluations		
implements policies and procedures with staff.	Y/N	Y/N
Supervisor's Comments:		

COMPANY SAMPLE FORM #1
Downloadable Form 5.1 *(Continued)*

2. Leadership The employee:	Employee Self-Rating	Supervisor Rating
fosters and sets high standards for his/her employees		
effectively delegates, ensures that employees are clearly and properly directed		
sets an example in terms of vision, confidence, and integrity		
Acts as a role model		
initiates change when necessary, encourages others to accept change		
Supervisor's Comments:		

3. Communication and Feedback The employee:	Employee Self-Rating	Supervisor Rating
provides constructive feedback to his/her employees		
is a good listener		
is accessible to his/her staff		
performs meaningful, timely, and collaborative performance evaluation with his/her employees		
communicates organizational goals, values, appropriate business updates		
exhibits foresight in recognizing potential problems and develops solutions		
Supervisor's Comments:		

Downloadable Form 5.2 has the following unique characteristics:

- A 5-point rating scale for General Skills, Job-Specific Skills, Management Skills, and Overall Performance.
- A 3-point rating scale to evaluate the degree of completion of current goals.
- An opportunity to rate an item "Not Applicable" if the manager does not have enough information (N/A is only available when rating General and Management Skills).
- Five General Skills plus one Management Skill to evaluate. Employees are rated on specific items under each competency and not on the overall competency. All employees are rated on the same competencies (management, only if applicable).
- The Job-Specific Skills section, where the items are specifically customized to each employee.
- The Current Goals section, with space to include the goals, a rating of completion, and any comments or examples.
- Only one box for all comments about General Skills, Job-Specific Skills, and Management Skills (can be found immediately after the rating of Overall Performance).
- Space for Future Goals at the end of the form.

COMPANY SAMPLE FORM #2*
Downloadable Form 5.2

Performance Review

Employee Name: _____   Supervisor Name: _____

Part I-A. General Skills: Please check the box that best represents the employee's performance on each skill, using N/A only for those that are not ratable due to lack of information.

General Skills	Exceptional	Above Average	Satisfactory	Needs Development	Unsatisfactory	N/A
Communication:						
Shares and disseminates information						
Listens openly and attentively						
Writes clearly and effectively						
Is clear and articulate in oral communication						
Work Management:						
Demonstrates ability to multitask and set priorities						
Manages projects to completion						
Uses available resources effectively						
Follows through without prompting						
Thinking and Problem Solving:						
Demonstrates creativity and innovation						
Identifies and solves problems effectively						
Thinks strategically						
Demonstrates sound judgment and decision-making						
Teamwork:						
Develops and maintains positive relationships						
Works collaboratively in group situations						
Values diverse points of view						
Helps develop peers and coworkers						

*To customize this document, download to your hard drive from www.wiley.com/go/PerformanceAppraisalForms. The document can then be opened, edited, and printed for personal use only, using Microsoft Word or another popular word processing application.

(continued)

COMPANY SAMPLE FORM #2
Downloadable Form 5.2 *(Continued)*

Individual Effectiveness:						
Takes initiative and is proactive						
Acts with professionalism and integrity						
Is adaptable and flexible						
Performs well under pressure						
Uses organized approach to job responsibilities						
Is attentive/responsive to needs of internal and/or external clients						
Takes ownership and holds oneself accountable						

Part I-B. Job-Specific Skills: This section covers critical job skills not included in section I-A. These may include specific business knowledge, technical skills, creative skills, etc. List each skill and check the box that best represents the employee's performance on each skill. Use the comments box at the end of Part III for summary, supporting statements, and recommendations for improvement and growth.

Job-Specific Skills	Exceptional	Above Average	Satisfactory	Needs Development	Unsatisfactory

Part I-C. Management Skills: To be completed *only* for those employees who manage direct reports. Please check the box that best represents the employee's performance on each skill, using N/A only for those that are not applicable. Use the comments box at the end of Part III for summary, supporting statements, and recommendations for improvement and growth.

Management Skills	Exceptional	Above Average	Satisfactory	Needs Development	Unsatisfactory	N/A
Builds and leads teams						
Defines, directs, and delegates work						
Communicates effectively with staff						
Creates positive and inclusive work environment						
Develops people through feedback and coaching						

COMPANY SAMPLE FORM #2
Downloadable Form 5.2 *(Continued)*

Part II. Current Goals: List employee's goals for the review period that just ended and indicate degree of completion with a checkmark. Use the Comments/Examples boxes for explanations, supporting statements, examples, etc.

Goals	Degree of Completion			Comments/Examples
	Fully	Partially	Not at All	
1.				
2.				
3.				
4.				
5.				

Part III. Summary of Overall Performance: Please check the box that best represents the employee's overall performance. Use the following comments box for summary, supporting statements, and recommendations for improvement and growth.

Exceptional	Above Average	Satisfactory	Needs Development	Unsatisfactory

Part IV. Future Goals: Supervisor and employee together should determine 3 to 5 goals for next year, taking into consideration department/corporate needs, employee's growth, and areas that need development.

	Goal	Completion Measurement	Time Frame (e.g., mid year, year end)
1.			
2.			
3.			
4.			
5.			

Downloadable Form 5.3 has the following unique characteristics:

- It has a 5-point rating scale for evaluating performance on Key Responsibilities and determining the Overall Rating.

- It provides the opportunity to select "Unratable" in evaluating a set of responsibilities/expectations if the employee is too new to receive a meaningful rating.

- A listing of the Company Mission and Department Goals is the first part of the form.

- The form is completely customized for each employee in the following way: Key Responsibilities and Performance Expectations against those responsibilities are decided on at the beginning of the year and are included on the form; employees are rated as to how well they met these expectations over the course of the year using the 5-point scale.

- No general, companywide competencies are included for evaluation; each employee's form is unique to his/her responsibilities and expectations.

- There is only one place for Supervisor Comments, immediately before the rating of Overall Performance. A space for Employee Comments is also included.

COMPANY SAMPLE FORM #3*

Downloadable Form 5.3

EMPLOYEE PERFORMANCE EVALUATION FORM

EMPLOYEE'S NAME: DEPARTMENT:

SUPERVISOR'S NAME: JOB TITLE:

COMPANY MISSION:

DEPARTMENT GOALS::

KEY RESPONSIBILITY	**PERFORMANCE EXPECTATION**

RATING:

_____ OUTSTANDING   _____ EXCEEDS EXPECTATIONS   _____ ACHIEVES EXPECTATIONS

_____ NEEDS DEVELOPMENT   _____ UNSATISFACTORY   _____ UNRATABLE

KEY RESPONSIBILITY	**PERFORMANCE EXPECTATION**

RATING:

_____ OUTSTANDING   _____ EXCEEDS EXPECTATIONS   _____ ACHIEVES EXPECTATIONS

_____ NEEDS DEVELOPMENT   _____ UNSATISFACTORY   _____ UNRATABLE

KEY RESPONSIBILITY	**PERFORMANCE EXPECTATION**

RATING:

_____ OUTSTANDING   _____ EXCEEDS EXPECTATIONS   _____ ACHIEVES EXPECTATIONS

_____ NEEDS DEVELOPMENT   _____ UNSATISFACTORY   _____ UNRATABLE

*To customize this document, download to your hard drive from www.wiley.com/go/PerformanceAppraisalForms. The document can then be opened, edited, and printed for personal use only, using Microsoft Word or another popular word processing application.

(continued)

COMPANY SAMPLE FORM #3
Downloadable Form 5.3 *(Continued)*

EMPLOYEE PERFORMANCE EVALUATION FORM

EMPLOYEE'S NAME: _____

Supervisor's Comments:

OVERALL RATING (SELECT ONLY ONE):

_____ OUTSTANDING   _____ EXCEEDS EXPECTATIONS   _____ ACHIEVES EXPECTATIONS

_____ NEEDS DEVELOPMENT   _____ UNSATISFACTORY   _____ UNRATABLE

RATINGS DEFINITION:

Outstanding: The employee consistently far exceeds the necessary job.

Exceeds Expectations: The employee exceeds the necessary job standards.

Achieves Expectations: The employee, because of his/her own efforts, attains all of the necessary job standards.

Needs Development: The employee's performance does not meet one or more of the attainable job standards.

Unsatisfactory: The employee's performance consistently does not meet several of the critical job standards.

Unratable: The employee being rated is too new to receive a meaningful rating.

Employee's Comments:

Downloadable Form 5.4 has the following unique characteristics:

- A 5-point rating scale is used for Job-Specific Skills, Companywide Skills, Management Skills, and Overall Performance.

- Job-Specific Skills are customized by job. Managers can choose the competencies relevant to their employees' roles from a broader list of competencies. These competencies change by role and can be customized even further with the addition of specific Job/Technical skills.

- Five Companywide Skills are included on every form; all employees, regardless of role, department, or level are evaluated on these same skills.

- Four Management Skills are included on every form; all managers, regardless of department or level are evaluated on these same skills.

- For each of the rating sections, managers evaluate the employees on broader competencies, each of which is defined on the form; individual behavioral items are not included for ratings on the form.

- Comments are divided into two boxes after all ratings except the overall rating; the two comment boxes cover the employee's areas of strength and areas of development.

- Descriptions of all points on the rating scale are included when the rating scale is presented for a final time for the evaluation of overall performance; managers can rate the employee as "New to Firm," meaning that s/he could receive feedback from other parts of the form but was too new to receive an overall rating.

- There is a section on Current Goals, with space to include the goals, a rating of completion, and any comments or examples.

COMPANY SAMPLE FORM #4*

Downloadable Form 5.4

| *To be completed by the Manager* | Year-End Performance Evaluation | Confidential |

EMPLOYEE NAME:_____	DATE OF EVALUATION: _____
DEPARTMENT: _____	DATE OF HIRE: _____
TITLE: _____	MANAGER'S NAME: _____

JOB SPECIFIC SKILLS (customized by job)	Far Exceeds Standards	Exceeds Standards	Meets Standards	Meets Some Standards	Does Not Meet Standards
COMMUNICATION – Transmits information clearly, in writing or verbally					
CUSTOMER SERVICE – Always puts the client first and does what's needed to meet their needs					
JOB KNOWLEDGE – Has all required knowledge needed for the job and consistently works to gain more					
PROBLEM SOLVING – Analyzes problems successfully and presents thoughtful solutions					
PROJECT MANAGEMENT – Manages projects to deadlines, budgets and resources					
Job/Technical Skill…					
Job/Technical Skill…					
Job/Technical Skill…					

COMPANY-WIDE SKILLS	Far Exceeds Standards	Exceeds Standards	Meets Standards	Meets Some Standards	Does Not Meet Standards
INNOVATION – Looks for new ways to improve					
LEADERSHIP – Provides vision and motivation in his/her role					
PROFESSIONALISM – Acts as a stellar representative of the company by always following policies and procedures					
QUALITY and PRODUCTIVITY - Produces as much work as possible with no tolerance for errors					
TEAMWORK – Collaborates with all parties (peers, seniors, directs and clients) to achieve goals					

*To customize this document, download to your hard drive from www.wiley.com/go/PerformanceAppraisalForms. The document can then be opened, edited, and printed for personal use only, using Microsoft Word or another popular word processing application.

COMPANY SAMPLE FORM #4
Downloadable Form 5.4 *(Continued)*

MANAGEMENT SKILLS *(if applicable)*	Far Exceeds Standards	Exceeds Standards	Meets Standards	Meets Some Standards	Does Not Meet Standards
MANAGING CHANGE – Explains changes to group and maintains performance throughout					
MANAGING INFORMATION – Communicates correct information to the correct parties					
MANAGING OTHERS – Supports and grows staff; manages performance appropriately					
MANAGING THE FUTURE – Keeps a big picture view and drives group to achieve it					

EMPLOYEE'S MAIN AREAS OF STRENGTH:

EMPLOYEE'S MAIN AREAS OF DEVELOPMENT:

(continued)

COMPANY SAMPLE FORM #4
Downloadable Form 5.4 *(Continued)*

Please rate the employee's overall performance for the year:

Far Exceeds Standards	☐	Job performance both far exceeds standards and makes a very significant contribution to the success of the department and the division.
Exceeds Standards	☐	Above-average job performance which both exceeds standards and makes a significant contribution to the success of the department and the division.
Meets Standards	☐	Job performance consistently meets and sometimes exceeds standards as well as makes a contribution to the success of the department and the division. The individual is fully functioning at the appropriate level.
Meets Some Standards	☐	Performance meets the minimum standards of the job, but is somewhat below the expected level. The employee's contribution to the success of the department and the division is minimal.
Does Not Meet Standards	☐	Job performance is completely unsatisfactory. The employee is consistently unable or unwilling to meet standards. A need for immediate and substantial improvement is warranted.
New to Firm	☐	Employee is too new to the firm to receive an overall rating.

EMPLOYEE COMMENTS:

Downloadable Form 5.5 has the following unique characteristics:

- Both managers and employees fill in data on this form.

- A 5-point rating scale is used for evaluating Targets and Results (all of Part I) and overall competency ratings in Part II.

- Part I represents a summary of yearlong performance against targets; the year-end form will be prepopulated with Performance Measures and the prior three quarters' targets, results, comments, and overall ratings.

- Both the manager and the employee fill out the data in Part I (Targets and Results); both parties work together to fill out the Performance Measures at the beginning of the year, as well as the targets for every quarter; employees fill in the results against every target and add comments at the end of every quarter; managers add their own comments and a rating for every quarter, plus the final rating against results achieved.

- The individual pages of Part I are divided up by Focus (Client, Business, Financial, etc.).

- Data in Part II (Individual Skills and Abilities) are also filled out by both the manager and the employee; the employee evaluates him/herself against individual behavior items under general competencies; the employee uses a 3-point scale to make this rating; the employee then provides examples to support his/her rating. The manager rates the employee on the same items, using the same scale and also can provide comments on every item. The manager also provides an overall rating for each competency as a whole. These overall ratings use the previous 5-point rating scale.

- All employees are evaluated against the same skills and abilities in Part II.

- Comments are made against each item; there is no space for general comments. There is also no overall rating.

COMPANY SAMPLE FORM #5*

Downloadable Form 5.5

Performance Year: _____   Employee Name: _____

Department / Role: _____   Location: _____

Manager: _____

Part I: Targets and Results

A. Client Focus

Performance Measure		1st Quarter Targets and Results	2nd Quarter Targets and Results	3rd Quarter Targets and Results	Year-End Targets and Results
	Target:				
1.	Result:				
	Target:				
2.	Result:				
	Target:				
3.	Result:				
	Target:				
4.	Result:				
	Target:				
5.	Result:				
Comments:		Comments:	Comments:	Comments:	Comments:

Rating Scale: Q1 Rating: Q2 Rating: Q3 Rating: Final Rating:

1 = Unacceptable   2 = Below Normal Level Performance   3 = Normal Level Performance

4 = High Level Performance   5 = Top Level Performance

---

*To customize this document, download to your hard drive from www.wiley.com/go/PerformanceAppraisalForms. The document can then be opened, edited, and printed for personal use only, using Microsoft Word or another popular word processing application.

COMPANY SAMPLE FORM #5
Downloadable Form 5.5 *(Continued)*

Performance Year: _____   Employee Name: _____

Department / Role: _____   Location: _____

Manager: _____

Part I: Targets and Results

B. Business Focus

Performance Measure		1st Quarter Targets and Results	2nd Quarter Targets and Results	3rd Quarter Targets and Results	Year-End Targets and Results
	Target:				
1.	Result:				
	Target:				
2.	Result:				
	Target:				
3.	Result:				
	Target:				
4.	Result:				
	Target:				
5.	Result:				
Comments:		Comments:	Comments:	Comments:	Comments:

Rating Scale: Q1 Rating: Q2 Rating: Q3 Rating: Final Rating:

1 = Unacceptable   2 = Below Normal Level Performance   3 = Normal Level Performance

4 = High Level Performance   5 = Top Level Performance

(continued)

COMPANY SAMPLE FORM #5
Downloadable Form 5.5 *(Continued)*

Performance Year: _____   Employee Name: _____

Department / Role: _____   Location: _____

Manager: _____

Part I: Targets and Results

C. Financial Focus

Performance Measure		1st Quarter Targets and Results	2nd Quarter Targets and Results	3rd Quarter Targets and Results	Year-End Targets and Results
	Target:				
1.	Result:				
	Target:				
2.	Result:				
	Target:				
3.	Result:				
	Target:				
4.	Result:				
	Target:				
5.	Result:				
Comments:		Comments:	Comments:	Comments:	Comments:

Rating Scale: Q1 Rating: Q2 Rating: Q3 Rating: Final Rating:

1 = Unacceptable   2 = Below Normal Level Performance   3 = Normal Level Performance

4 = High Level Performance   5 = Top Level Performance

COMPANY SAMPLE FORM #5
Downloadable Form 5.5 *(Continued)*

Part II: Individual Skills and Abilities

Employee Instructions: Provide a rating and supporting examples for each of the items listed below, based on last year's performance.

Manager Instructions: Provide a rating and comments for the employee for each of the items listed below, based on his/her self-evaluation, short-term evaluations (provided separately), and personal observation. Also provide an overall rating for each of the categories, using the 1-5 scale from Part I.

	Selected Self-Rating: Exceeds Target, on Target, or Needs Improvement	Example(s) to Support Self-Assessment	Manager's Rating and Comments
Communication			
Writes clearly and accurately			
Speaks clearly and articulately			
Communicates effectively to all groups			
Keeps people in the loop			
			Overall Rating:
Self-Development			
Actively seeks opportunity to receive feedback			
Keeps up with current trends and practices			
Attends trainings, conferences, etc. in the field			
			Overall Rating:
Teamwork			
Meets own responsibilities on the team			
Helps others with their responsibilities			
Gets along with all team members			
			Overall Rating:

PART III

READY-TO-USE, DOWNLOADABLE, CUSTOMIZABLE EVALUATION STATEMENTS

CHAPTER 6

Twenty-One Top Core Competencies and Four Managerial Competencies

Instructions for Using These Forms

1. Find the competency or competencies for which you need to write a description of an employee's performance.

2. Log on to the Wiley web site to retrieve electronic versions of all of these competencies.

3. Cut or copy the text from the appropriate level of performance in our book and paste it onto your form.

4. Edit the text for the following elements:

   a. Replace all placeholders (e.g., [xxxx], s/he, him/her) with the data appropriate for the employee (e.g., the employee's name and appropriate gender pronoun). These placeholders are all noted by the presence of brackets [   ].

   b. Delete or change any parts of the text that are not applicable to the employee whom you are currently evaluating. For instance, the text may make reference to external customers when the employee you are evaluating only has internal customers. Simply modify the text to reflect this fact and continue on.

   c. Add examples specific to the particular employee to supplement the text from the book. These examples can either be woven into the text itself or provided at the end, after the prompting phrases we have provided (e.g., "Specific examples of when [xxxx] showed exceptional flexibility and multitasking were . . .").

5. Do a final proofread of all text to make sure every statement is accurate for the employee's performance.

6. Repeat process for all remaining competencies and for all employees.

Twenty-One Top Core Competencies

ACCOUNTABILITY, RESPONSIBILITY, AND DEPENDABILITY*
Downloadable Form 6.1

Exceeded Expectations

[   ] exceeded expectations in the areas of accountability, responsibility, and dependability last year.

Accountability and Responsibility

In any situation, [   ] could be counted on to accept accountability for [his/her] own decisions, actions, or results. When problems arose, [s/he] did not play the "blame game" but instead would perform a fair analysis of the issue to try to unearth its causes. Whatever the reason(s) behind the problem, [s/he] would take responsibility for the consequences of the actions in the past and own the responsibility for making all appropriate changes in the future.

If [   ] ever made any errors in the work [s/he] did, [s/he] immediately acknowledged and apologized for them. [S/he] then attempted to turn the mistakes into positives by using them as data for learning how to improve in the future. [S/he] encouraged this attitude of accountability as the basis for continual improvement throughout the whole department.

In any project [   ] was involved in, [s/he] would take possession of work as [his/her] own. [S/he] adopted a "buck stops here" attitude for all of [his/her] work, and as such, clients and colleagues looked at [him/her] as a person to go to for help. As questions arose, [s/he] would use all available resources to find an answer and never slough off the responsibility to someone else on the team without appropriate supervision and communication.

[   ] was given the maximum level of responsibility for someone in [his/her] role and then even went beyond these levels to take on more responsibility as [s/he] got involved in different projects. [S/he] eagerly accepted formidable challenges and for even the most complex situations would never say "that's not my job."

When [   ] delegated work, [s/he] remained accountable for the final results, and [s/he] communicated this fact to the person to whom [s/he] was delegating as well as to the client. [S/he] always made [him/herself] available for questions and help along the way and knew when to step in and take back a level of responsibility, if needed for the final quality of the work product.

(continued)

ACCOUNTABILITY, RESPONSIBILITY, AND DEPENDABILITY
Downloadable Form 6.1 *(Continued)*

Dependability

[   ] was a model of dependability last year and showed this characteristic in a variety of situations.

[S/he] could always be counted on to complete assignments or deliver on promises. [S/he] did not miss a single deadline over the whole year. [His/her] dependability did not apply only to single tasks. For example, when [s/he] delivered one part of an assignment, [s/he] would then move on to complete the next step, often turning in work products in advance of their due dates. [   ] was exemplary in [his/her] follow-through. [His/her] actions were always consistent with what [s/he] said she would do, and in fact, more often than not, [s/he] would go above and beyond [his/her] original commitments. There were no instances of when [s/he] went back on [his/her] word.

In team settings, [s/he] could be relied on to complete the responsibilities outlined for [his/her] part of the project. In addition, whenever possible, [s/he] would finish [his/her] tasks and then move on to help other team members with their tasks.

[   ] was extremely dependable in [his/her] daily actions. [S/he] always showed up on time for meetings and turned in all of [his/her] work on time as well. When [s/he] had a crucial role in a meeting or project, [s/he] typically would respond by exceeding expectations on dependability. If [s/he] was the facilitator for a meeting, [s/he] would show up extra early; if [his/her] work was needed before anyone else on the team could progress in their responsibilities, [s/he] would make sure it was done as soon as possible. [   ] was always fully prepared with [his/her] work.

[   ] was able to maintain this dependable behavior even in times of crisis or great complexity. In fact, in any situation, [   ] actions over the past year were those of an extremely reliable, conscientious, and trustworthy employee.

ACCOUNTABILITY, RESPONSIBILITY, AND DEPENDABILITY
Downloadable Form 6.1 *(Continued)*

Specific examples of when [   ] showed exceptional accountability, responsibility, and dependability were:

_____

_____

_____

_____

_____

Met Expectations

[   ] met expectations in the areas of accountability, responsibility, and dependability over the past year.

Accountability and Responsibility

[   ] usually accepted accountability for [his/her] own decisions, actions, or results. When problems arose, [his/her] first reaction was not to fault other people or circumstances. Rather, [s/he] would attempt to analyze the issue to determine its causes. In general, [s/he] would own whatever the reason(s) for the problem were and attempt to address them. There were some instances, where [s/he] shifted the blame to another person—either internal or external—or situation and said it was outside [his/her] control.

If [   ] committed any errors in [his/her] work, [s/he] generally acknowledged and apologized for them, although this did not always happen immediately. [S/he] also tended to adopt an attitude of accountability as a necessary evil rather than a challenge [s/he] enthusiastically adopted and tried to learn from.

In the projects [   ] was involved in, [s/he] took possession of work expressly assigned to [him/her] as [his/her] own. For this work, [s/he] was extremely responsible and worked hard to complete it correctly. If questions arose on these tasks, [s/he] would look to find an answer. However, this accountability did not extend beyond preassigned tasks, and as such [s/he] was seen as a "go to" person only for a small area of responsibility. For anything outside this scope, [   ] would not answer questions from clients or colleagues, even if maintaining this silo approach to work came at the expense of the project.

(continued)

ACCOUNTABILITY, RESPONSIBILITY, AND DEPENDABILITY

Downloadable Form 6.1 *(Continued)*

[   ] was given an appropriate level of responsibility for someone in [his/her] role. [S/he] embraced this level of responsibility but did not look to take on more.

When [   ] delegated work, [s/he] tried to remain accountable for the final results, although there were some examples—typically in more stressful or complex situations—when [s/he] handed off this accountability to a more junior person without proper support or communication. In these cases, if the final quality of the work product was compromised, [s/he] did not fully acknowledge [his/her] role in that result.

Dependability

[   ] was a mostly dependable employee last year. In general, [s/he] could be counted on to complete assignments or deliver on promises. [S/he] met most deadlines last year, although there were a few that [s/he] did not meet. [S/he] was most dependable on a task-by-task basis. That is, when [s/he] was given an assignment, [s/he] could generally be counted on to follow through to completion and finish the task according to the guidelines and time frames established. What [   ] did not show, however, was any exceptional behavior or proactivity in regard to these tasks. [S/he] was not known for finishing tasks in advance, looking for more challenging tasks, or helping others with their tasks.

[   ] exhibited average follow-through skills. For the most part, [s/he] would do what [s/he] said [s/he] would. However, [his/her] actions would not go beyond these commitments. Also, there were a couple of instances where [s/he] went back on [his/her] word. This seemed to happen mostly when [   ] was feeling overloaded or stressed with work. In these cases, though, [s/he] did not communicate to the relevant parties that [s/he] would not be able to meet their expectations, thus resulting in some unnecessary conflicts.

[   ] saw the need for dependability in team settings. [S/he] could be relied on to complete the responsibilities outlined for [his/her] part of the project, although these responsibilities were generally on the basic side.

[S/he] tried to show up on time for meetings and turn in [his/her] work on time as well. [S/he] did better at this when [s/he] had a crucial role in a meeting (e.g.,

ACCOUNTABILITY, RESPONSIBILITY, AND DEPENDABILITY
Downloadable Form 6.1 *(Continued)*

facilitator) or project (e.g., needed to kick off workflow). If [s/he] perceived [his/her] role as not as crucial, [s/he] would slack off from being quite as dependable. For instance, if [s/he] did not see the purpose of [his/her] presence at a meeting, [s/he] might choose not to attend and at times would do this without informing the other parties. For the most part, [   ] showed up prepared with [his/her] work.

In summary, [   ] actions over the past year were those of a moderately reliable, conscientious, or trustworthy employee. One could count on [him/her] to do the job that was specifically outlined for [him/her] but should not expect anything more.

Specific examples of when [   ] showed accountability, responsibility, and dependability were:

_____

_____

_____

_____

_____

_____

Specific examples of when [   ] failed to show accountability, responsibility, or dependability were:

_____

_____

_____

_____

_____

_____

_____

(continued)

Did Not Meet Expectations

[   ] did not meet expectations in the areas of accountability, responsibility, and dependability last year.

Accountability and Responsibility

Over last year, [   ] repeatedly did not accept accountability for [his/her] own decisions, actions, or results. When problems arose, [s/he] would always look to point the blame elsewhere. These candidates for blame could be other people—either internal such as coworkers or external such as vendors—or they could be circumstances that [s/he] said [s/he] could not control—such as computers breaking down or other technology not working.

[   ] would not make [him/herself] answerable to any errors that occurred in the work [s/he] did. [S/he] did not create an environment where employees acknowledged mistakes and learned from them. Instead, [s/he] would always look outside to find fault in someone or something other than [him/herself]. Even when there were not problems but just questions about [   ] work, [s/he] would try to skirt the issue. [S/he] would not take possession of work as [his/her] own but rather attempt to diffuse responsibility to the larger team. This resulted in great frustration on the part of colleagues or clients who needed clear, final answers to questions.

[   ] was given the minimal level of responsibility for someone in [his/her] role. There were no examples of when [s/he] looked to take on further responsibility.

In situations when [   ] delegated [his/her] work, [s/he] would remove [him/herself] from any part of the responsibility for that work, even if [s/he] was ultimately responsible for the results. Instead, [s/he] would let the person who completed the work be accountable for any errors, even if that person was extremely junior and had to complete the work without assistance.

Dependability

Last year, [   ] showed that [s/he] could not be depended on in numerous situations. As a rule, [s/he] could not be counted on to complete assignments or deliver on promises. When [s/he] would deliver on one piece of an assignment, [s/he] could not dependably complete the next step or perform any sort of follow-through. This lack of dependability was true even if [   ] expressly said [s/he]

ACCOUNTABILITY, RESPONSIBILITY, AND DEPENDABILITY
Downloadable Form 6.1 *(Continued)*

would do something. There were many instances where [s/he] went back on [his/her] word or on commitments [s/he] made in either a verbal or written form. [His/her] actions were not consistent with what [s/he] said.

In team settings, [s/he] could not be counted on to complete the responsibilities outlined for [his/her] part of the project. If at all possible, [s/he] would slough off [his/her] tasks to another team member. [S/he] was not viewed by colleagues or clients as reliable.

This lack of dependability applied to regular, daily tasks. [   ] had great problems showing up on time for any meetings or turning any work in on time. This was true even if [his/her] performance or data was crucial to the meeting or project. [S/he] would be late to meetings even if [s/he] was the facilitator and would miss a task deadline, even if [his/her] work was needed before anyone else on the team could progress in their responsibilities. [   ] was rarely fully prepared with [his/her] work in any situation.

This undependable behavior got worse in crises or complex situations. In these instances, even with explicit instructions and constant check-ins, [   ] would miss deadlines or turn in haphazard work or work that was largely different from that which was required. In some instances, [s/he] simply checked out and failed to complete any part of [his/her] expected work.

Overall, [   ] actions over the past year were not those of a reliable, conscientious, or trustworthy employee.

Specific examples of when [   ] failed to show accountability, responsibility, or dependability were:

_____

_____

_____

_____

_____

_____

ANALYTICAL THINKING AND PROBLEM SOLVING*
Downloadable Form 6.2

Exceeded Expectations

Last year, [   ] exceeded expectations in the area of analytical thinking and problem solving.

[S/he] was able to look at a mass of data and see distinct relationships as well as glean what was the most important point or issue. [His/her] analyses were consistently done quickly but without sacrificing quality, which was always stellar and showed insight above and beyond what was expected. [   ] used a very methodical approach in [his/her] analyses and yet was able to adjust this methodology to the needs of the situation and look beyond the "off-the-shelf" solutions. This deliberate yet customized methodology meant that [   ] analyses were consistently right on the mark. [His/her] analyses were always purposeful and showed evidence of strategy and big picture thinking in their formulation.

[   ] was also able to present the results of [his/her] analyses in the format that the audience would find most useful. In these results, [s/he] provided just enough detail that the audience would get all the information needed and quickly see the bottom line conclusions, without getting lost in all the data.

[   ] applied [his/her] strong analytical skills to solving problems with complete success. [S/he] identified the information needed to solve the problem and was able to obtain this information, even if it involved looking outside [his/her] immediate resources. Then, [   ] worked to quickly assess the problem and get to the core issues. [S/he] was able to identify trends or gaps and pull out the salient causes rather than just looking at the surface symptoms. [S/he] also was quick to tap into [his/her] past experience as well as the experience of others in attempting to find the best solution.

[   ] was very creative in [his/her] problem-solving efforts. [S/he] would start with an educated approach to the problem, but if this approach was not successful, [s/he] rapidly changed gears to something that would work. This did not happen often, however, as [   ] did an excellent job anticipating potential problems and developing appropriate contingency plans.

[   ] always looked beyond the current problem [s/he] was dealing with to see how it linked with or could be affected by other issues. [S/he] understood the full

impact of the problems [s/he] dealt with, and this big picture thinking contributed to the success of the solutions [s/he] developed. [S/he] was also able to deal with multiple issues at once, including some of the most complex the group faced all year. All were resolved to the satisfaction of each party involved, and with the knowledge that the solutions were robust and not Band-Aids applied merely to avert the immediate crisis.

Specific examples of when [   ] showed exceptional analytical thinking and problem-solving skills were:

_____

_____

_____

_____

_____

_____

_____

_____

Met Expectations

[   ] met expectations in the area of analytical thinking and problem solving over the past year. [S/he] was able to analyze most data and come up with recommendations. Likewise, [s/he] possessed the ability to solve most problems presented over the year.

In terms of analytical skills, [s/he] was typically able to look at a situation and apply an appropriate analytical approach using available methodologies and resources. [S/he] communicated the results of these analyses in a clear fashion and in a format that was easily understandable by and useful for the intended audience. [   ] usually completed these analyses without undue delays.

(continued)

ANALYTICAL THINKING AND PROBLEM SOLVING
Downloadable Form 6.2 *(Continued)*

There were a few instances where [   ] got into trouble with [his/her] analyses. This tended to happen when [his/her] initial approaches were not successful for some reason (due either to an incorrect assumption or to changing of data). When this happened, [   ] tended to struggle to regain [his/her] footing in the analytical process, and this often resulted in delays or mistaken conclusions. [S/he] also struggled with analyses a few times when the data was overly complex. In general, though, [s/he] met expectations in the ability to sort through the data and pull out the correct and relevant conclusions.

In problem solving, [   ] had several proven methodologies that [s/he] successfully applied to situations to come up with solid solutions. In these instances, [s/he] approached the process quickly and systematically to get to the core issues of the problem. [S/he] attempted to delve deeper than just the surface symptoms. [   ] used good judgment in dealing with these problems, and [his/her] recommended solutions tended to be robust.

[   ] tried to learn from past successes and failures. [S/he] knew when to escalate problems to the next level and when to bring in help. [S/he] attempted to anticipate potential obstacles and come up with ways to work around them, although these efforts were only partially successful.

Where [   ] really needed help in problem solving was in dealing with more complex situations. [S/he] had difficulty dealing with more than one problem at a time and also did not make an effort to look for solutions outside [his/her] box of available methods or resources. As such, [his/her] recommended solutions were often simply adequate and did not display any creativity or attempt to impact broader issues.

Specific examples of when [   ] showed good analytical thinking and problem-solving skills were:

_____

_____

_____

_____

Specific examples of when [   ] needed improvement in analytical thinking and problem-solving skills were:

_____

_____

_____

_____

Did Not Meet Expectations

[   ] did not meet expectations in the area of analytical thinking and problem solving last year. [His/her] reasoning skills and ability to find solutions were severely lacking.

[   ] did not display the skills needed to analyze situations. [S/he] would often not be able to complete anything beyond the most basic interpretation of a situation and would often draw incorrect conclusions from even the most basic analyses. In general, [his/her] studies of situations or problems would not be detailed enough.

In the instances when [s/he] did complete more detailed analyses, these analyses focused on the unimportant aspects of a situation; [   ] could not pull out the most salient points of a set of data but rather would get stuck in "analysis paralysis." In these situations, [   ] would gather tons of information that [s/he] was unable to sort into any useful framework for use by another party. [His/her] analyses covered many more pages than was necessary, and after reading these reports, the audience would still be left looking for the clear conclusion.

This lack of analytical skills was even more profound when [   ] needed to apply these skills to solving problems. [S/he] had difficulty in all phases of problem solving. Up front, [s/he] did not identify what information was needed to solve a problem, and thus was often left having to scramble to obtain more (or more appropriate) data.

(continued)

ANALYTICAL THINKING AND PROBLEM SOLVING
Downloadable Form 6.2 *(Continued)*

Once [   ] had the data [s/he] thought necessary, [s/he] would still be unable to analyze the problem using any sort of a logical or systematic approach. [S/he] did not make quick diagnoses, and even after lengthy examination, [his/her] recommended approach to the problem often seemed to address only part of the issue. [S/he] looked only at the symptoms of the problem rather than attempting to find and deal with any underlying causes. [   ] did not examine the problem from numerous angles and would tend to use only the facts and resources in [his/her] world rather than looking around for more creative solutions. If [his/her] initial solution did not work, [   ] had great difficulty changing course and coming up with another solution.

[   ] unsuccessful approach to problem solving failed to improve after coaching. [S/he] did not learn from past mistakes and was not proactive in trying to prevent current problems from occurring again. [S/he] continued to fail to see where to bring in external help or escalate issues, even when [s/he] was not making progress toward a solution on [his/her] own.

In all instances, [   ] was only able to deal with the problem at hand, again, usually unsuccessfully. [S/he] could not deal with more than one problem at once and had extra difficulty dealing with complex issues. There were no examples of where [s/he] was able to look beyond the current problem to see the bigger picture—either proposing unique solutions or making links to problems from other areas.

Specific examples of when [   ] showed poor analytical thinking and problem-solving skills were:

_____

_____

_____

_____

_____

_____

_____

_____

_____

COMMUNICATION*
Downloadable Form 6.3

Exceeded Expectations

Last year, [   ] exceeded expectations in the area of communication. [S/he] articulated concepts and positions effectively in both written and oral communications.

[   ] communicated effectively to coworkers more senior, junior, or at the same level as [him/her]self. [S/he] communicated equally well with people in [his/her] immediate department as [s/he] did with those in other groups or external to the company. [   ] could analyze the audience and adjust [his/her] message to meet their needs and styles. This resulted in clear communications that successfully reached their targets and met [   ] goals whether they were to persuade, update, or simply inform.

In terms of verbal communications, [   ] presented information clearly and succinctly. [S/he] used strong body language and vocal factors to make [his/her] message more impactful. [S/he] also delivered [his/her] messages with confidence and conviction and consistently did a good job responding to any questions or concerns from various audiences. [S/he] displayed strong verbal skills both when delivering formal, prepared talks as well as when [s/he] spoke on an impromptu basis. [   ] also asked thoughtful and purposeful questions, which often served to broaden the scope of a discussion. In general, [s/he] was able to get the audience involved in [his/her] presentation of ideas. [   ] showed these verbal skills in all settings, from formal meetings to one-on-ones. [S/he] was also equally successful when verbal communications had to be conducted via video or teleconference; [   ] made sure to adapt [his/her] message and style to the limitations of the technology.

[   ] showed that [s/he] knew when written communications would be more appropriate than verbal ones and was able to convey a positive, persuasive impression solely through the written word. In written communications, as with verbal ones, [s/he] presented information in a clear, succinct, and effective manner. [S/he] employed an understandable structure in these communications and included the amount of detail appropriate for the audience. [   ] also always took the time to proofread all written documents, thus minimizing any spelling or grammar errors. [S/he] was so strong in [his/her] editing skills that [s/he] often

---

(continued)

COMMUNICATION
Downloadable Form 6.3 *(Continued)*

reviewed documents for others on the team to help make their writing more effective.

Equally important to outward communications, [   ] also managed the other side of the communication cycle extremely well. [S/he] displayed excellent listening skills and over the past year always took the time to make sure [s/he] understood other people's points of view in conversations. [S/he] listened to any ideas or feedback provided by others. [S/he] was able to maintain this empathic listening even when dealing with people who were upset.

In short, [   ] was an exemplary communicator last year. In all communications, [s/he] conveyed a positive image of [him/herself], [his/her] team, and the company. [His/her] messages often served to provide valuable insight and necessary direction to their audiences. [S/he] was able to maintain this success when communicating either the greatest of successes or the most difficult of news items. [His/her] strength in communication served as a model to team members, and [s/he] frequently worked with others to fine-tune their messages. In general, [   ] fostered a general air of open communication in the group.

Specific examples of when [   ] showed exceptional communication were:

Met Expectations

[   ] met expectations in the area of communication over the past year. For the most part, communications were delivered in a clear and concise manner, yet there are some areas of development for [him/her] to focus on.

[   ] seemed to be most successful at communication when communicating to an audience that was similar to [him/her]. There were many instances when [s/he] delivered a message to a peer in [his/her] department that was organized, understandable, and effective. [S/he] was less effective in being able to adapt [his/her] communication to different audiences. This applied both in terms of level (e.g., more senior or junior) or just a different style (e.g., more or less direct, more or less detail, etc.).

[   ] also seemed to be better in terms of communications where the goal was simply to inform a group about something than when it was necessary to persuade the audience or deliver bad news. In these more complicated communications, [   ] message often got muddled, and the audience's needs or concerns were not as thoroughly addressed.

For the most part, [   ] was a good public speaker. [S/he] did not have any distracting body language or vocal habits, and [s/he] was able to display confidence about [his/her] message. [S/he] was not remembered as a particularly effective or engaging speaker, however. [S/he] tended to simply deliver [his/her] message and stop rather than attempt to engage the audience and bring them into [his/her] presentation. [   ] tended to do better when presenting basic or prepared messages. There were times when [s/he] struggled to effectively convey more complicated ideas or answer questions "off the cuff." [   ] handled verbal communications via technology (e.g., video or teleconference) with no problems.

[   ] was also able to convey [his/her] ideas clearly in written formats. [S/he] attempted to follow an organized structure in [his/her] writing, although at times [s/he] abandoned this structure, which resulted [him/her] creating a muddled written message. For the most part, [s/he] provided the right amount of detail in [his/her] writing, although there were instances where a lack of detail left the reader confused or the preponderance of detail left the reader overwhelmed. In general, [   ] documents contained few spelling and grammar errors.

(continued)

COMMUNICATION
Downloadable Form 6.3 *(Continued)*

[   ] listening skills last year were average. [S/he] knew that [s/he] should be listening to the other party in a communication, and typically made an effort in that regard. However, too often, the listening would be at the surface level only (e.g., with head nods or "uh huhs" only), rather than using any active listening skills that would display true empathy or desire to understand the other party's message. [S/he] did better at listening when [s/he] had the time to do so than when [s/he] was busy and did better when [s/he] liked what [s/he] was hearing than when [s/he] disagreed with the speaker's message.

Overall, [   ] displayed average communication skills last year. [S/he] met the basic expectations in [his/her] communications but failed to show any inspiration or extra energy behind the messages [s/he] delivered on behalf of [him/herself], [his/her] team, or the company. [His/her] communications did not serve as models for others, nor did they shut down the atmosphere of open communication among the group.

Specific examples of when [   ] showed good communication skills were:

_____

_____

_____

_____

_____

_____

Specific examples of when [   ] showed poor communication skills were:

_____

_____

_____

_____

_____

_____

_____

COMMUNICATION
Downloadable Form 6.3 *(Continued)*

Did Not Meet Expectations

[   ] did not meet expectations in the area of communication last year. [S/he] was not able to articulate concepts and positions effectively in either written or oral communications.

[   ] had trouble communicating to a variety of audiences and in a variety of ways. When communicating with people more senior than [him/her], [s/he] would frequently provide them with too much detail and could not synthesize "the bottom line" or link [his/her] message to broader business goals. When communicating with peers, [s/he] again could not deliver a clear, succinct message and would waste time focusing on [his/her] own needs rather than attempting to develop a collaborative, give-and-take communication process. When communicating with people more junior than [him/her], [   ] would often adopt a condescending tone and made no attempt to answer questions. [   ] also did extremely poorly in communications with people outside [his/her] department or outside the company. In all these instances, [   ] failed to accurately read the communication styles of [his/her] audience or make any adaptations to this style, and at times these missteps in communication were serious enough as to damage relationships and reputations.

[   ] was largely unsuccessful in [his/her] verbal communications. [S/he] did not establish credibility with the audience and typically did not speak with conviction about [his/her] ideas. As such, [   ] ability to persuade was severely hampered. [   ] also did not display strong body language or vocal traits in [his/her] presentations, and examples such as having slouching posture, poor eye contact, and a monotone or overloud voice often hurt the effectiveness of [his/her] message. [S/he] made no attempt to engage the audience and bring them into the presentation through the use of questions or other interactive skills. [S/he] was equally ineffective with planned or impromptu presentations and also struggled with the use of communicating through technology such as video or teleconferences.

[   ] written communications were also poor. [His/her] stream-of-consciousness style reflected no attempt to structure the document to make it easier for the reader to digest, and the typical numerous grammar and spelling mistakes showed that [s/he] did not take the time to proofread [his/her] work.

(continued)

COMMUNICATION
Downloadable Form 6.3 *(Continued)*

[   ] also did not meet expectations in terms of being a good listener. [S/he] would frequently interrupt other parties when they were talking and seemed to take no interest in any ideas voiced other than [his/her] own. This lack of listening would occur both in one-on-one settings and in large group meetings. [   ] listening skills were particularly poor when [s/he] did not agree with the speaker's message—[s/he] had no tolerance for discussions that included any differences of opinion and would cut off or disengage from these discussions, often in a rude and abrupt manner.

In short, [   ] displayed extremely poor communication skills last year. [S/he] did not seem to be able to deliver any type of message— short or long, good news or bad, in a written or oral format or to any type of audience—in an effective manner. [His/her] poor communication skills were so severe that they shut down the goal of open communication in the broader team, and instead served as a gag effect for the entire group, where no one felt comfortable discussing new or controversial ideas.

Specific examples of when [   ] showed poor communication skills were:

CREATIVITY*
Downloadable Form 6.4

Exceeded Expectations

[   ] exceeded expectations in the area of creativity. Over the past year, [s/he] consistently came up with new ideas and valuable insights that resulted in a fresh way of looking at something. [S/he] was viewed by others to be ingenious and innovative in numerous ways.

[   ] consistently demonstrated creative thinking in a variety of situations. If there was a problem, [s/he] developed new ways of approaching it until arriving at a creative solution that typically reached beyond what anyone had thought of before. [S/he] was able to display this originality in problem solving even for the most challenging of issues. [S/he] did not let obstacles get in the way of [his/her] creative problem solving. In fact, when barriers to [his/her] original plans arose, [   ] bumped up the level of creativity and came up with even more original ideas or solutions. A great way that [   ] creativity manifested itself was in [his/her] resourcefulness.

In addition to demonstrating creativity in problem solving, [   ] fostered an atmosphere of innovative thinking and applied this type of thinking to any situation. [S/he] always looked for new ideas and approaches and chose to question the tried-and-true rather than continuing to do things simply because "they've always been done that way." [S/he] was completely open to experimentation and willing would listen to and try any new idea or alternate solution that was appropriate and within established guidelines.

The fact that [   ] demonstrated creativity on a regular basis, rather than just on isolated projects or problems, contributed to the outstanding rating for this competency. Another testament to the strength of [   ] creativity was that [s/he] promoted a creative climate and inspired the rest of the team to be creative. [S/he] frequently sought new approaches on [his/her]own and encouraged others to do the same by welcoming all ideas.

Through all of these efforts, [   ] established an environment in which creativity flourished for [him/herself] and the rest of the team. [   ] made sure that these imaginative efforts did not work only on paper, however. [S/he] ably translated the creative thinking into real changes and solutions that advanced the efforts of the department and the company.

(continued)

CREATIVITY
Downloadable Form 6.4 *(Continued)*

Specific examples of when [   ] showed creativity were:

_____

_____

_____

_____

_____

Met Expectations

[   ] met expectations in the area of creativity over the past year. There were several instances when [s/he] came up with creative ideas or solutions, and at times [s/he] came up with new insights that contributed to more effective outcomes than would have been reached without this originality of thought.

In terms of problem solving, [   ] thought in a creative manner when specifically directed to do so by [his/her] manager. For example, in structured brainstorming sessions, [s/he] would contribute imaginative and unique ideas, several of which were actually implemented over the course of the year. [S/he] would not necessarily come up with these ideas unless asked, however, and did not always see the need for creative thinking on [his/her] own. In trying to implement [his/her] creative ideas, [   ] had difficulties if any barriers occurred. It often seemed as if [his/her] imaginative thinking had been used up at the beginning of the problem-solving process. At the first sign of resistance, [s/he] reverted back to the old, standard way of doing things rather than continue [his/her] innovative thinking to create workarounds to obstacles.

[S/he] was not known for being overly resourceful, although again, could usually come up with some version of a solution when pressed. There were times when [   ] imagined a very creative solution that had other problems that [s/he] did not see, such as not falling into established guidelines or not being realistic in the work world.

[   ] creativity seemed to suffer under tight deadlines or times of stress. It was noted that all the examples of creative thinking occurred in slower periods or when [s/he] was working only on one project. In contrast, when time was of the

CREATIVITY
Downloadable Form 6.4 (Continued)

essence or [s/he] needed to multitask, [s/he] rarely showed creativity. In these situations, [   ] tended to default to the typical ways of doing things, even if this was not the ideal course of action. In general, [   ] showed a moderate level of openness to experimentation.

There were a few instances when [   ] was found to be open to creativity in [his/her] coworkers. However, again, these instances tended to occur when [s/he] felt there was time to listen to new ideas. If time was tight, this space for creative discussions and brainstorming was not seen as a high priority. [S/he] rarely sought new approaches by [him/herself] and only moderately encouraged others to do experiment on their own.

On [his/her] own, [   ] did not establish an environment in which creativity flourished but for the most part, [s/he] did not resist innovation for the team.

Specific examples of when [   ] showed creativity were:

_____

_____

_____

_____

_____

Specific examples of when [   ] failed to show creativity were:

_____

_____

_____

_____

_____

(continued)

CREATIVITY
Downloadable Form 6.4 *(Continued)*

Did Not Meet Expectations

[   ] did not meet expectations in the area of creativity. [S/he] displayed a level of creativity below that which is required by the job. [S/he] rarely, if ever, came up with new ideas on [his/her] own, either for solving a problem or improving a process. Even when asked to come up with new ideas, [   ] only displayed dull, unimaginative thinking.

[   ] did not engage in creative problem solving, even when specifically directed to do so by [his/her] manager. In structured brainstorming sessions, [s/he] would rarely make contributions, imaginative or not. There were no examples of a new idea from [   ] being implemented over the course of the year. When forced to engage in creative thinking, [s/he] would make a halfhearted attempt to come up with new ideas or solutions, but in reality these were mostly restatements of already established thinking. In any case, the minute any obstacles arose to these "new" ideas, [   ] would use these barriers as an excuse to revert to the original way of doing things. Alternatively, however, there were examples of when [   ] had thought [s/he] came up with an incredibly creative solution to a problem, but [his/her] idea was so outrageous (e.g., costing way too much in terms of time or money) that it would never work in the "real" world.

[   ] did not exhibit any examples of resourcefulness over the course of the year. [S/he] had a limited toolbox of solutions that [s/he] pulled from as needed and did not show any desire to tweak these tools or get new ones. [   ] showed an apparent fear of any change from the status quo and would stay blindly committed to the original process or plan, at the expense of continuous improvement. [S/he] was entirely inflexible when presented with improvement suggestions, which was particularly troublesome when the status quo was broken and improvements were greatly needed.

CREATIVITY
Downloadable Form 6.4 *(Continued)*

Also troublesome was that [   ] not only failed to exhibit creativity [him/herself], but [s/he] also discouraged it in others. [S/he] definitely preferred thinking "inside the box." In fact, whenever ideas arose in team meetings that [s/he] considered outside the box, [s/he] would dismiss them as too radical and extreme, frequently hampering the brainstorming process. [S/he] had no tolerance for experimentation and would get paralyzed by the risks and the "what ifs" of what could go wrong with new ideas. When presented with new ideas [s/he] had to implement, [s/he] would only do so after great protest, which had the effect of stifling of imaginative thinking across the group. [   ] resistance to innovation hurt the creative progress of the entire team.

Specific examples of when [   ] failed to show creativity were:

_____

_____

_____

_____

_____

_____

_____

CUSTOMER FOCUS*
Downloadable Form 6.5

Exceeded Expectations

[   ] exceeded expectations in the area of customer focus last year. This high level of customer service was seen in all stages of [his/her] dealing with the customers and in dealing with all types and levels of customers or clients—both internal and external.

In beginning any work with a customer, [   ] was extremely clear in defining expectations for the work and the relationship. [S/he] made it clear to the customers that they were building a long-term relationship together and treated each new issue as an opportunity to develop a close, working partnership. [S/he] did this with every type of customer relationship—including external customers as well as people [s/he] considered internal customers in the company. These internal customers received [   ] same high level of customer focus as a more traditional customer outside the organization.

As work with the customers proceeded over the year, [   ] first and foremost met all established commitments. [S/he] always kept the clients in the loop about the work and would respond to any needs, requests, or questions immediately and without complaint. In addition, [   ] consistently exceeded customers' expectations about the work, often coming back with improvements and enhancements the customers did not foresee. [   ] took the time to learn and keep updated on the working worlds of [his/her] customers and used this information to go above and beyond expected service levels. [S/he] was incredibly knowledgeable about [his/her] customers worlds and was often complimented for knowing as much or more about their work as they did.

When changes arose, [   ] made sure to modify the approach as needed and advise the customers of any alterations to plans well in advance. If problems ever arose, [   ] always put the customer first and looked for ways to solve the problems that were in the best interest of the customer. In these problem solving situations, [   ] never lost [his/her] cool or got annoyed with the customers. Even when customers contacted [him/her] and were upset, [   ] kept [his/her] own emotions in check and found a way to calm them down while at the same time gleaning a solution that worked for all without harming the relationship. There were no instances when a incident with one of [   ] customers got out of control and had to be referred to someone else for resolution.

[   ] is a model of customer focus excellence. [S/he] he is extremely valued by [his/her] customers, many of whom have provided feedback on the excellent work [s/he] did over the past year. These customers are overwhelming loyal to [   ].

Specific examples of when [   ] showed customer focus were:

_____

_____

_____

_____

_____

_____

_____

_____

_____

_____

Met Expectations

[   ] met expectations in the area of customer focus over the past year. [S/he] was usually competent in [his/her] dealings with customers and was seen as professional in these interactions.

[   ] did [his/her] best to assess customer needs in advance of a project. [S/he] asked questions to complete these assessments, although these questions were typically at a very basic level and rarely served to uncover unique customer needs or issues beyond the obvious ones.

[   ] attempted to build long-term relationships with [his/her] customers. Again, these relationships were based on a steady level of standard service, which

CUSTOMER FOCUS
Downloadable Form 6.5 *(Continued)*

customers appreciated. What was missing from [   ] customer focus was any attempt to "wow" customers with any unexpected, value-adding ideas or offerings. Commitments to the customers were consistently met, although not exceeded. [S/he] was aware that customer focus applied to internal as well as external dealings.

[   ] attempted to keep customers informed on the status of work and projects on an ongoing basis. The only time this did not seem to occur was during times of stress or change. In these instances, [   ] tended to default to doing things without consulting [his/her] customers and even in a couple of instances snapped at customers when [s/he] perceived they were asking too many questions or "getting in the way." Also, it was in these more difficult times that [   ] missed some client deadlines, although in general, [his/her] timeliness and client responsiveness were on target.

When a customer issue arose, [   ] did [his/her] best to resolve it in a timely manner. In solving these problems, [s/he] attempted to keep [his/her] cool and focus on calming down the client. [S/he] was typically successful in these endeavors, although again there were a couple of instances when [s/he] got hooked and responded sharply. For the most part, though, [   ] was committed to fixing whatever the problem was and keeping relationship with the customer intact.

In general, [   ] put the client's needs first and was dedicated to meeting those needs in a timely manner. Customers reported that they enjoyed working with [   ] and that [s/he] did a good job.

Specific examples of when [   ] showed customer focus were:

CUSTOMER FOCUS
Downloadable Form 6.5 *(Continued)*

Specific examples of when [   ] failed to show customer focus were:

_____

_____

_____

_____

_____

_____

_____

_____

Did Not Meet Expectations

Over the past year, [   ] did not meet expectations in the area of customer focus. Rather than modeling a "customer is always right" mentality, [   ] would instead frequently either confront or ignore [his/her] customers and [s/he] viewed their presence as more of an annoyance that had to be dealt with than as a group of people [s/he] tried to please.

[   ] failed to build relationships—either short- or long-term—with [his/her] customers. [   ] conducted interactions on the purely transactional level. No attempt was made to develop partnerships or shared accountability on any projects or processes. There were no examples where [s/he] went out of [his/her] way to please [his/her] customers, nor did [his/her] customers make any effort to do anything special for [   ]. [   ] had particular trouble understanding the idea of an internal customer; [s/he] did not think customer service needed to apply to anyone within the company.

[   ] failed to accurately assess the needs of [his/her] customers. [S/he] was not knowledgeable about the core things [his/her] customers cared about but made assumptions about their needs based on [his/her] own opinions. As such, [s/he] frequently delivered work that was unacceptable to customers. Additionally, [   ] missed many deadlines for [his/her] customers. [S/he] often delivered work in piecemeal fashion or not at all. Promises were consistently broken and follow-up on customer concerns was sporadic or nonexistent.

(continued)

CUSTOMER FOCUS
Downloadable Form 6.5 *(Continued)*

[   ] customers often reported feeling out-of-the-loop in working with [him/her]. [   ] did not establish ongoing communication with [his/her] customers and would undercommunicate both in the areas of regular status updates as well as updates for critical incidents. [S/he] got annoyed when customers asked what [s/he] considered to be too many or too "stupid" questions and replied with a sharp tone of voice or simply did not reply at all. In fact, there were several examples where [   ] had to be reprimanded for [his/her] inappropriate tone with customers, which could range from impolite to condescending to downright angry.

[   ] handled customer problems especially poorly. [S/he] typically delayed in acting on such issues, which made the problem worse and the customer more upset. [   ] failed to successfully calm down these irritated customers, and more often than not these situations had to be referred to someone higher up for resolution. Such situations were damaging to not only [   ] reputation but to the company's reputation as well.

Several complaints were made about [   ] lack of customer focus over the course of the year; however, this feedback was ignored and no improvements were seen. [S/he] currently has no loyal customer base. The overall level of customer satisfaction in [   ] performance last year was extremely low.

Specific examples of when [   ] failed to show customer focus were:

_____

_____

_____

_____

_____

_____

_____

_____

_____

DECISION MAKING AND JUDGMENT*
Downloadable Form 6.6

Exceeded Expectations

[   ] exceeded expectations in the areas of decision making and judgment last year. [S/he] excelled in all aspects of the decision-making process, including identifying which decisions needed to be made and then making them effectively. [S/he] consistently exercised excellent judgment in these and other activities.

[   ] easily and accurately entered into the decision-making process. [S/he] quickly recognized when a process or discussion had stalled such that it needed a decision to move it to the next level and worked to summarize the issues and put a decision on the table in these situations. [S/he] was able to call for or make decisions in situations without detailed instructions or when the decision had to be made without all the desired information. [   ] was completely comfortable making decisions independently, yet at the same time, [s/he] knew when to call in others as appropriate or needed. In making decisions, [s/he] would poll relevant other parties to get their inputs and ideas, but [s/he] was able to be the "bottom-line" decision maker, remaining firm and accountable for the chosen course of action.

When it came to actually making decisions, [   ] also displayed strong performance. [S/he] avoided making hasty decisions, and instead relied consistently on using a strong, rational decision-making process. In this process, [s/he] consistently started by setting a clear goal for the decision. [S/he] gathered all the facts and circumstances relevant to the decision. [S/he] then carefully analyzed these facts and circumstances and worked to simplify the decision by identifying key information and criteria for making assessments. [S/he] always considered all alternatives before making any commitments and clearly outlined the strengths and weaknesses of each. [   ] did a particularly good job of assessing risk in decision making. [S/he] always examined the consequences and costs of various alternatives before making any decisions. After conducting all these analyses, [   ] reported feeling comfortable that [s/he] was making a sound, well-thought out, and well-justified decision. These decisions were also frequently innovative and resourceful, due to the amount of time spent examining different options.

[   ] did especially well dealing with critical or high-pressure decisions. [S/he] exuded confidence in these situations and was able to successfully balance the

---

*Copyright © 2006 by Swan Consultants, Inc. To customize this document, download to your hard drive from www.wiley .com/go/PerformanceAppraisalForms. The document can then be opened, edited, and printed for personal use only, using Microsoft Word or another popular word processing application.

(continued)

DECISION MAKING AND JUDGMENT
Downloadable Form 6.6 *(Continued)*

strong foundations of [his/her] decision-making procedure against the high stakes or time pressure of these decisions. The decisions [s/he] made under high-stress circumstances were consistently sound. In addition, [   ] showed that [s/he] could make and stand by unpopular decisions, if [his/her] decision-making process showed these choices to be the strongest in the long run. [   ] goal was always to make the right choice, not the one that would be the easiest or most popular.

Not only did [   ] make effective decisions on [his/her] own, [s/he] also was effective in leading a team decision process. In these situations, [s/he] made sure to consider all the "people sides" to decision making: ensuring that everyone participated in the discussion and that they were listened to and supported in their ideas. At the same time, [s/he] was on guard for groupthink, and made sure that differences of opinion were allowed to surface, so that all sides of the issue were examined. [S/he] successfully reconciled conflicting views as part of the decision-making process. [   ] strength in these skills meant that [s/he] was frequently asked to lead team decision-making sessions and asked to make broad decisions affecting larger business groups.

[   ] displayed many other sophisticated skills of decision making. [S/he] considered both the short- and long-term views and consequences in making decisions. [S/he] also evaluated the effects different options would have on people internal and external to the group. [S/he] effectively balanced risk, return, complexity, and speed in making decisions. [S/he] was also able to balance the needs of multiple parties involved in the same decision. [S/he] tried to unearth any hidden issues that could impact decisions. Overall, [   ] was viewed as an excellent decision maker last year; the choices [s/he] made or led teams to make were seen as consistently sound, rational, and on target.

Additional to the strengths [   ] exhibited in decision making, [s/he] also displayed a more general strength with [his/her] judgment skills. [S/he] approached almost any situation with an open mind, and where [s/he] had a preformed idea, these judgments were made based on a through consideration of facts rather than on rumor or "gut feelings." As a rule, [   ] formed sound conclusions based on careful consideration. [S/he] repeatedly showed excellent judgment in dealing with people at all levels from clients to staff to more senior managers. [S/he] served as a role model in [his/her] assessment skills and discouraged others on the team from making preformed or uninformed judgments, encouraging instead an atmosphere of open-mindedness.

DECISION MAKING AND JUDGMENT
Downloadable Form 6.6 *(Continued)*

Specific examples of when [   ] showed exceptional decision-making and judgment abilities were:

_____

_____

_____

_____

Met Expectations

[   ] met expectations in the areas of decision making and judgment over the past year. [S/he] functioned at a satisfactory level with most aspects of the decision-making process, including identifying which decisions needed to be made and then actually making them effectively. [S/he] generally exercised good judgment in these and other activities.

[   ] satisfactorily completed activities at the beginning of the decision-making process. [S/he] recognized when a process or discussion had stalled such that it needed a decision to move it to the next level. When pushed, [s/he] was able to call for or make decisions in situations without detailed instructions or when the decision had to be made without all the desired information. [S/he] was not comfortable in these instances, however, and at times delayed making decisions in these less-than-ideal conditions, even when these delays were not optimal. [   ] attempted to make decisions independently, although [s/he] was really only at ease doing this for decisions where [s/he] had high levels of expertise. For decisions where [s/he] was less informed, [s/he] repeatedly polled other parties (whether or not they were relevant) for their opinions and needed to get advice from [his/her] manager before taking any action, thinking that this would help mitigate the risk of any criticism [s/he] would garner as a result of a bad decision.

For more standard, routine decisions or again, for those where [s/he] had a lot of expertise, [   ] did a good job making [his/her] choice and then standing firm and in support of this choice, even in the face of opposition. For tougher, more complex decisions, however, [   ] would try to postpone having to commit to one course of action. Even after committing, [   ] would have trouble remaining supportive of [his/her] choice. In a few of these instances, [   ] went back on decisions [s/he] had made, only to later change back to [his/her] original choice as sentiments about the topic changed.

(continued)

DECISION MAKING AND JUDGMENT
Downloadable Form 6.6 *(Continued)*

When it came to actually making decisions, [   ] also displayed an average level of performance. [S/he] tried to avoid making hasty decisions and instead relied on a considered decision-making process, although [s/he] did not use this process consistently. [S/he] started by gathering the facts and circumstances relevant to the decision. [S/he] then analyzed these facts and circumstances and worked to simplify the decision by identifying key information and criteria for making assessments. This process was typically successful, although it was not as powerful as it could have been because [   ] frequently forgot to pay attention to the bigger-picture goal of the decision. This resulted in too much time being spent analyzing unnecessary information. [   ] considered multiple alternatives before making any commitments and attempted to outline the strengths and weaknesses of each. This was again mostly successful, although there were typically one or two alternatives [s/he] did not consider, and as such the resulting options were not exceedingly innovative or resourceful. [   ] also analyzed the consequences and costs of various alternatives before making any decisions.

After conducting all these analyses, [   ] would feel comfortable that [s/he] was making a sound, well-thought out, and well-justified decision. This was often true, although there were a few instances where the analyses were incorrect or incomplete, and the final decision was compromised as a result.

[   ] was not as strong in dealing with critical or high-pressure decisions. [S/he] attempted to use [his/her] same decision-making process in these situations, but [s/he] lacked confidence in making these decisions, and this timidity affected the assessment process. In these instances, [s/he] would either be too rigid, insisting on following the traditional path of previous decisions when the situation called for more creative thinking, or [s/he] would unpredictably choose a path without providing a clear rationale.

[   ] displayed a mixed amount of some of the more sophisticated skills of decision making. [S/he] attempted to consider both the short- and long-term views and consequences in making decisions. [S/he] tried to consider the effects different options would have on people internal and external to the group. [S/he] looked to balance risk, return, complexity, and speed in making decisions. [S/he] also tried to balance the needs of multiple parties involved in the same decision. In each of these instances, the motivation was there, and sometimes the ability followed, but there was not a consistency in [his/her] behavior.

DECISION MAKING AND JUDGMENT

Downloadable Form 6.6 *(Continued)*

[   ] did a better job making effective decisions on [his/her] own than in leading teams' decisions. In team settings, [s/he] tried to consider the "people sides" to decision making, for example, ensuring that everyone participated in the discussion and that they were listened to and supported in their ideas. In several instances, however, these efforts fell short, and [s/he] either simply imposed [his/her] view on the group or let "group think" take over, resulting in making the easy choice without a thorough examination of different thoughts and opinion. [S/he] also had trouble reconciling conflicting views as part of the decision-making process.

Beyond decision making, [   ] displayed a satisfactory level of judgment skills. [S/he] approached most situations with an open mind and tried to reserve final judgments until hearing all the facts. [S/he] avoided judgments made on rumors or "gut feelings". [S/he] attempted to use good judgment in dealing with people at all levels from clients to staff to more senior managers and for the most part was successful. There were some instances, however, where [s/he] misread a situation and [his/her] judgment suffered accordingly. This tended to happen when [s/he] judged things too quickly or was under stress.

Specific examples of when [   ] showed strong decision-making and judgment abilities were:

_____

_____

_____

_____

Specific examples of when [   ] failed to show strong decision-making and judgment abilities were:

_____

_____

_____

_____

_____

(continued)

DECISION MAKING AND JUDGMENT
Downloadable Form 6.6 *(Continued)*

Did Not Meet Expectations

[   ] did not meet expectations in the areas of decision making and judgment last year. [S/he] had problems with many aspects of the decision-making process, including identifying which decisions needed to be made and then actually making them effectively. [S/he] continuously failed to exercise good judgment in these and other activities.

[   ] had difficulty entering into the decision-making process. [S/he] could not easily recognize when a process or discussion had stalled such that it needed a decision to move it to the next level. [S/he] also often had problems feeling as if [s/he] had enough information to make a decision, and as such did not take any actions to arrive at a resolution, even when action was crucial. When it was obvious that a decision had to be made, [   ] was uncomfortable making decisions independently. Rather, [s/he] repeatedly polled other parties (whether or not they were relevant) for their opinions and needed to get advice from [his/her] manager before taking any action, thinking that this would help mitigate the risk of any criticism [s/he] would garner as a result of a bad decision.

Especially with tough decisions, [   ] would try to postpone having to commit to one course of action, and even after committing, [s/he] would have trouble remaining supportive of [his/her] choice. [S/he] had no problems going back on decisions [s/he] had made, only to flip back to [his/her] original choice again later as sentiments about the topic changed.

When it came to actually making decisions, [   ] also displayed poor performance. [S/he] often made hasty decisions, in which [s/he] failed to evaluate all the facts and circumstances carefully. [S/he] lacked a plan on how to identify key information and the criteria for making assessments. [S/he] also did a poor job of considering different options in the decision-making process and examining the strengths and weaknesses of each. In fact, [   ] did a particularly poor job of assessing risk in regard to decision making. [S/he] tended to ignore the consequences and costs of poor decisions, choosing often the more popular option, rather than what would have the greatest benefit in the long run. In general, [   ] resisted making unpopular decisions, even when they were the correct ones.

[   ] did especially poorly dealing with critical and/or high-pressure decisions. [S/he] lacked confidence in making these decisions, and this timidity affected the assessment process. In these instances, [s/he] would either be too rigid, insisting

DECISION MAKING AND JUDGMENT
Downloadable Form 6.6 *(Continued)*

on following the traditional, often uninspired path of all previous decisions, or [s/he] would unpredictably choose a path without providing a clear rationale.

[   ] did not display any of the more sophisticated skills of decision making. [S/he] did not consider both the short- and long-term views and consequences in making decisions. [S/he] also did not consider the effects different options would have on people internal and external to the group. [S/he] did not balance risk, return, complexity, and speed in making decisions. [S/he] was also not able to balance the needs of multiple parties involved in the same decision. [S/he] never attempted to unearth any hidden issues that could impact decisions. [S/he] had difficulty reconciling conflicting views as part of the decision-making process. [S/he] never was asked to make broad decisions affecting larger business groups.

All these factors resulted in [   ] avoiding making decisions, even when it was absolutely imperative. When [s/he] did finally make decisions, they were frequently poor and ineffective.

Additional to the problems [   ] exhibited in decision making, [s/he] also displayed more general issues with poor judgment. [S/he] approached almost any situation with [his/her] opinion already firmly set, and often these judgments were made based on rumor or mistaken "gut feelings" versus on facts. [S/he] did not form sound conclusions based on careful consideration. [S/he] repeatedly showed poor judgment in dealing with people at all levels from clients to staff to more senior managers. Even when instructed specifically to do so (as in a brainstorming session) [   ] found it very difficult to approach situations with an open mind.

Specific examples of when [   ] failed to show strong decision-making and judgment abilities were:

_____

_____

_____

_____

_____

_____

_____

_____

ETHICS AND STANDARDS*
Downloadable Form 6.7

Exceeded Expectations

[   ] exceeded expectations in the area of ethics and standards last year. [S/he] not only met all established guidelines in these areas but championed them to others and helped develop even more robust guidelines.

[   ] demonstrated a firm commitment to the standards set for the department. [S/he] maintained this commitment even during times of high stress or major change. As needed, [s/he] would lead the effort for adapting the standards to new demands or requirements.

[S/he] was also seen as a role model for ethical behavior within the group. [   ] showed [him/herself] to be scrupulously honest in all activities. [S/he] was able to maintain this integrity even in times of conflict or when the consequences had a negative effect on [him/herself]. [S/he] also addressed any issues of ethics [s/he] observed with [his/her] colleagues. [S/he] addressed these infringements from a coaching mentality, rather than an offensive "stick to the rules" mentality, which resulted in behavior change without damage to working relationships.

[   ] made an effort to always stay up-to-date on any changes in ethics or standards (e.g., qualifications or certifications) in the industry. [S/he] proactively would pass on these updates to the team, making sure that the department's standards were always the most advanced.

[   ] always treated confidential information with the utmost respect and never sacrificed this confidentiality for matters of personal gain or convenience.

All these efforts resulted in [   ] gaining the highest level of respect both with colleagues and clients (internal and external). Colleagues consulted [   ] on questions of standards and ethics, and clients repeatedly praised [   ] for [his/her] fair dealings, again, even in times of stress.

ETHICS AND STANDARDS
Downloadable Form 6.7 *(Continued)*

[   ] actions over the course of the year represented the highest level of ethical behavior possible. [S/he] not only behaved within standards and ethics for [him/herself] but coached others on this behavior. In addition, she was committed to helping the entire organization establish and maintain the highest possible ethics and standards for the work they produce and relationships they develop.

Specific examples of when [   ] showed exceptional ethics and standards were:

_____

_____

_____

_____

_____

_____

Met Expectations

[   ] met expectations in the area of ethics and standards over the past year. [S/he] demonstrated knowledge of the policy and procedure standards for the group and attempted to apply them at all times. [S/he] also demonstrated knowledge of the ethics behind the work [s/he] completed and tried to stay within these ethical boundaries at all times.

[   ] displayed honesty and integrity in the work that [s/he] did over the course of the year. When presented with a moral dilemma, [s/he] would attempt to do the right thing. [S/he] was very conscious of the importance of correctly handling confidential information and did [his/her] best to follow procedure with this information.

(continued)

ETHICS AND STANDARDS
Downloadable Form 6.7 (Continued)

While [   ] met the basic expectations around standards and ethics, [s/he] would not be called a role model for this behavior in that [s/he] did not work to develop the practices of standards or ethics within the department or broader organization. [S/he] tended to treat dealing with standards and ethics as something to check on a list and did not keep an open eye as to how these practices could or should be advanced in light of changes in the work or industry. Also, while [s/he] was very mindful of exhibiting ethical behavior [him/herself], [s/he] shied away from encouraging or coaching this behavior in others. Even in examples with the most blatant disregard of standards, [   ] did not address the issue with others.

Over the course of the year, [   ] completed all the requirements for ethical behavior and met the established standards with [his/her] work. However, [s/he] did not look to develop any new guidelines in these areas, and while there were no complaints about the integrity of [his/her] actions, neither were there any compliments from colleagues or clients.

Specific examples of when [   ] showed acceptable ethics and standards were:

_____

_____

_____

_____

_____

_____

Specific examples of when [   ] failed to show acceptable ethics and standards were:

_____

_____

_____

_____

_____

_____

ETHICS AND STANDARDS
Downloadable Form 6.7 *(Continued)*

Did Not Meet Expectations

[   ] did not meet expectations in the area of ethics and standards last year. There were several instances where [s/he] violated the ethical guidelines of the company, and these breaches of ethics resulted in repeated complaints from clients (internal and external) as well as from colleagues. [S/he] did not work to keep up to date with standard policies and procedures, and thus frequently went astray from these guidelines in [his/her] work.

In general, [   ] viewed adherence to the ethics and standards of the organization to be a matter of inconvenience. [S/he] would frequently bend these standards to suit [his/her] needs in a given situation and develop new processes or policies to accommodate [his/her] work. At times this meant looking for loopholes to get around regulations [s/he] did not want to comply with. In more serious instances, it meant overtly lying or misrepresenting data to others.

[   ] also had trouble maintaining the confidentiality of information. [S/he] was very lax in the treatment of this type of material and did not seem to grasp that compromising this information had potential effects not just on the person or group but on the company at large.

In some instances, [   ] would claim to not be aware of what the standards or ethics were in a given situation. However, even after being repeatedly briefed with the guidelines and told that they applied in every instance, [s/he] still frequently failed to meet them.

There were no instances when [   ] took the lead in establishing ethical guidelines or setting up standards for a group or project. [S/he] also never went outside the organization in attempt to educate [him/herself] as to what the ethics and standards were for the broader industry.

(continued)

ETHICS AND STANDARDS
Downloadable Form 6.7 *(Continued)*

In summary, [   ] did not behave within the guidelines set up by the department and organization last year. On several occasions, [s/he] flouted the standards established to provide a level of consistency and quality to the department's work. [S/he] also often compromised ethics with no apparent regard for the risk or consequences of these actions.

Specific examples of when [   ] failed to show acceptable ethics and standards were:

_____

_____

_____

_____

_____

_____

_____

_____

_____

FLEXIBILITY AND MULTITASKING*
Downloadable Form 6.8

Exceeded Expectations

Over the past year, [　　] exceeded expectations in the area of flexibility and multitasking. [S/he] showed [him/herself] to be extremely versatile and able to handle numerous tasks simultaneously, all with a high level of success.

[S/he] possessed many different skills, abilities, and knowledge areas and was able to pull upon these as needed to address the situation at hand. As such, [s/he] could perform a wide variety of tasks, all with a high level of efficiency and effectiveness. [　　] was also flexible in adapting [his/her] job role and was willing to change [his/her] current responsibilities and take on more responsibilities when asked.

[　　] showed instances of functioning successfully both as a generalist and a specialist last year. [S/he] provided experience, talent, and support in a wide breadth of areas and could always be asked to pitch in to deal with a pressing issue, whether [s/he] had the most experience in it or not. At the same time, [s/he] could work deeply in several diverse subject matters, learning and providing the high level of detail for a particular project or process.

[　　] effortlessly managed numerous projects at the same time. [S/he] set clear goals, time lines and priorities for each of [his/her] projects and used these preparations to plan [his/her] work flow around the different assignments. [S/he] moved seamlessly from one project to another, spending time on the most important factors and always managing to move each project ahead. Most impressively, [　　] exhibited this multitasking not just for [his/her] own activities but also for those of [his/her] teams or coworkers. [S/he] effectively managed the work of groups on multiple assignments simultaneously by leading any changes through clear planning, directions, and communication.

If changes arose in [　　] work, [s/he] dealt with these unpredictable conditions with ease. [S/he] displayed a positive mind-set toward any shifts in [his/her] work circumstances and would be open and flexible to changes rather than resentful or resistant. [S/he] realized that there were many different ways to deal with a given situation, and when called for, [s/he] could go "off process" and adapt to the current situation to successfully address a problem, time line shift, or other

(continued)

adjustment. Often, in fact, [s/he] was able to display this versatility even before it was overtly requested. [S/he] had a repertoire of diverse skills and tapped into what was necessary on a moment's notice to address the current need. [   ] showed this quick flexibility on a variety of topics, whether it was changes to the work or to the work setting (such as when or where it was done). At the last minute, [s/he] would be equally willing to adapt the procedure for completing a task as [s/he] would be to work late or on the weekend if that was what was needed.

[   ] showed this ability to be flexible and to multitask both when the changes or balancing of work came from [his/her] own doing as well as when it was imposed by others. On [his/her] own, [s/he] knew when to make changes to foster improvements and how to balance many projects at once. Yet in addition, [s/he] was also willing to try new ideas proposed by others and was able to effectively balance the needs of [his/her] work with requests from colleagues.

Specific examples of when [   ] showed exceptional flexibility and multitasking were:

_____

_____

_____

_____

Met Expectations

[   ] met expectations in the area of flexibility and multitasking over the past year. Under the right conditions, [s/he] showed [him/herself] to be versatile and able to handle numerous tasks simultaneously.

[   ] possessed a repertoire of different skills, abilities, and knowledge areas. [S/he] was able to tap into these areas as needed to address the situation at hand, although this flexibility was diminished if [s/he] needed to call on resources beyond what [s/he] had acquired. In addition, [   ] versatility tended to be confined to changes within [his/her] job role; she was not as willing or able to adapt when the adaptations involved changes or additions to [his/her] current responsibilities.

To a point, [   ] was able to manage several projects at the same time. When presented with this situation, [s/he] set goals, time lines, and priorities for each of the projects and used this preparation to plan [his/her] work flow around the

FLEXIBILITY AND MULTITASKING
Downloadable Form 6.8 *(Continued)*

different assignments. This resulted in successful multitasking, for the most part, although there were a few instances where a lack of clarity in the planning (e.g., in goals, time lines, or priorities) resulted in a confusion of work management. When the projects were of a controlled number, [   ] effectively moved from one project to another, attempting to focus on the most important factors and usually moving each project ahead. To be successful, however, [   ] ability to multitask needed to be planned and coordinated. If an unexpected glitch arose in one of [his/her] projects, or if a new task was added on, [   ] ability to optimally deal with each project was compromised.

[   ] could only multitask for [his/her] own activities. This ability did not expand to managing the complexities of various groups working on multiple assignments simultaneously.

In general, [   ] tried to be open and versatile to changes that arose. [His/her] first response was not to be resentful or resistant to change. In dealing with changes, [s/he] tried to be flexible and adapt how [s/he] was currently working to the new set of circumstances. [S/he] realized that there were many different ways to deal with a given situation, and when called for, [s/he] was able to go "off process" and adapt to the current situation to successfully address a problem, time line shift, or other adjustment. The instances where [   ] struggled with this flexibility were when [s/he] needed to respond to new situations rapidly. [S/he] often needed time to process any shifts in requirements or working circumstances, and when [s/he] didn't have this time, [s/he] would not be as versatile in [his/her] responses. [   ] tended to be more flexible when [s/he] saw change coming and understood its origins than when [s/he] had to adapt to new situations [s/he] didn't foresee or comprehend.

Finally, [   ] met expectations in the areas of flexibility and multitasking, but [s/he] was not necessarily consistent in these areas. At times, [s/he] was only able to display these abilities in limited areas. For instance, [s/he] could be flexible in changes to the work (changing a procedure or process) but not when it would get done (staying late unexpectedly to finish). Other times, [s/he] would have no problem coming in on the weekend for a last-minute need but would really push back against a change in how to complete a task, clinging instead to how it had always been done before. Regardless of the situation, [   ] showed a better ability to be flexible and multitask when the changes or balancing of work came from [his/her] own doing than when it was imposed by others. On [his/her] own, [s/he] was able to make adjustments designed to foster improvements and balance several projects at once, but [s/he] often was less open to trying new ideas

(continued)

proposed by others or juggling multiple demands if they arose from requests from colleagues.

Specific examples of when [   ] showed flexibility and multitasking were:

_____

_____

_____

_____

Specific examples of when [   ] failed to show flexibility and multitasking were:

_____

_____

_____

_____

Did Not Meet Expectations

[   ] did not meet expectations in the area of flexibility and multitasking last year. [S/he] did not show [him/her]self to be versatile nor able to handle numerous tasks simultaneously.

Over the course of the year, [   ] did not display a broad range of skills, abilities, or knowledge areas. Therefore, when a situation arose that required flexibility, [s/he] had a limited group of resources for responding to it. [S/he] did not seem to be motivated to adapt [his/her] job role to make it more versatile and was typically unwilling to change [his/her] current responsibilities or take on more responsibilities when asked. [   ] was a big proponent of the status quo. [S/he] liked things the way they were and tended to react negatively to anything that caused [him/her] to have to shift from that course.

[   ] had great difficulty managing more than one project at the same time. When presented with this situation, [s/he] was unable to set goals, time lines, and priorities for each of the projects. When [s/he] attempted these preparations, the results were often unclear and thus useless in helping plan [his/her] work flow around the different assignments. This resulted in unsuccessful multitasking for the most part, and this lack of success applied whether [s/he] was trying to balance several things at once or even when making a simple choice of which of two tasks to complete first. When faced with such decisions, [   ] would often

FLEXIBILITY AND MULTITASKING
Downloadable Form 6.8 *(Continued)*

become paralyzed and unable to do work on any project without some outside assistance in organizing the different tasks. Even with extensive coaching, if an unexpected glitch arose in one of the projects, or if a new task were added, [   ] work would freeze again, until [s/he] obtained help with the multitasking dilemma. [   ] shortcomings in the ability to multitask were so severe on an individual level, that there were no instances when [s/he] would have been ready to organize multiple tasks or projects for larger teams.

In general, [   ] was completely closed to any idea or suggestion of flexibility. [His/her] first response was to be resentful or resistant to change, and [s/he] showed no interest in why the change was occurring or what its possible needs or benefits might be. Rather than being flexible, [   ] tended to have to be dragged into changes kicking and screaming. [S/he] often refused to accept that there could be a new and better way to deal with a given situation, preferring instead to deal with the tried-and-true method, even when it was obvious that this traditional way of doing things was broken and no longer effective. When working on a team, [s/he] was not open to new ideas proposed by others and certainly did nothing to foster these discussions. On [his/her] own, [   ] was not able to go "off process" and adapt the current situation to successfully address a problem, time line shift, or other adjustment.

This inability to respond to change was true in any time frame whether [s/he] was asked to change on the spot or with months to prepare. [S/he] was also equally inflexible in response to changes to the work itself (e.g., changing a procedure or process) or to when it would get done (e.g., having to stay late unexpectedly to finish). [   ] had a method that [s/he] he liked and believed in for all the work that [s/he] did. When asked to deviate from that path, [s/he] would always push back. [S/he] would also be the last person to volunteer to work outside the daily routine and would have to be specifically ordered to change [his/her] work hours even if it was obvious that extra or different timing was what was needed to finish a job in a pinch. In general, [   ] would not make shifts in any part of [his/her] work until threatened with discipline, and even then would change only with great resentment and animosity.

Specific examples of when [   ] failed to show flexibility and multitasking were:

_____

_____

_____

_____

GOAL-ORIENTED AND DRIVE FOR RESULTS*
Downloadable Form 6.9

Exceeded Expectations

Last year, [   ] exceeded expectations in being goal-oriented with a drive for results. [S/he] did an outstanding job of setting appropriate goals and staying focused to ensure [s/he] achieved them.

In setting goals, [s/he] made sure to link them to the goals of the department and the larger company, such that [his/her] achievement of these targets contributed to significant advancement. [   ] excelled in the actual process of setting goals. All [his/her] goals followed the SMART formula: They were specific, measurable, achievable, relevant, and time-bound. [S/he] set appropriate goals for all [his/her] long-term projects and also for the short-term steps to outline the process for achieving these future objectives.

[   ] chose appropriate topics for [his/her] goals. The goals were created around significant targets, which were designed to move the work forward when they were achieved. [S/he] did not set goals around day-to-day or maintenance work that was already being easily achieved. [   ] goals were innovative yet also realistic. They were also easily communicated and were set in conjunction with [his/her] manager and [his/her] view of what should be accomplished over the year.

[   ] was so effective at setting goals, [s/he] was frequently asked to set team goals for the department and to help colleagues with the formulation of their goals.

Once [   ] goals were set, [s/he] used them as the driving force in [his/her] quest to obtain results. The results [s/he] wanted to achieve were outlined in the goals, and it was the effectiveness of the goal setting that allowed [   ] to maintain momentum in working to achieve the results.

The specificity, measurability, and time lines of [   ] goals allowed [him/her] to plan and organize the work and resources to have the best chance of achieving the desired results. The strong goals also helped [   ] to evaluate [his/her] progress over the year. If [s/he] ever found [him/herself] off track in pursuit of these goals, [s/he] was tenacious in tackling the obstacle until [s/he] got back on track. [S/he] showed [him/herself] to be extremely resilient in pursuit of [his/her] goals. [S/he] also was realistic, and if a goal turned out to be unachievable, [s/he] would adjust it accordingly.

GOAL-ORIENTED AND DRIVE FOR RESULTS
Downloadable Form 6.9 *(Continued)*

[   ] displayed a sense of urgency to achieve the outcomes [s/he] established at the beginning of the year. [S/he] was driven to achieve [his/her] targets and not easily discouraged in this quest. It was this diligence and persistence that contributed to [him/her] not just achieving but surpassing all the goals [s/he] set.

Specific examples of when [   ] showed [s/he] was goal-oriented with a drive for results were:

Met Expectations

Over the past year, [   ] met expectations in being goal-oriented with a drive for results. [S/he] set appropriate goals and showed the appropriate level of drive to achieve them.

[   ] understood at a basic level how [his/her] goals fit in with those of the department and organization. Therefore, in setting goals, [s/he] attempted to tie them back to the bigger picture. [S/he] did this with mixed success; some goals had an obvious link to larger-scale targets, whereas others were not as relevant. [   ] attempted to follow the SMART formula with her goals to make them specific, measurable, achievable, relevant, and time-bound. For most goals, [s/he] was able to meet some of these criteria but not all. For example, some did not include a way to evaluate whether [s/he] was making progress against the goal (measurable); some were either too easy or too difficult (achievable), and others did not include any deadlines (time-bound).

[   ] included a mix of time frames (both long-term and short-term) in [his/her] goals. However, there were some long-term goals that did not include enough short-term subgoals to help plan work flow and resources, and there were several short-term goals that did not link up to any longer-term results.

[   ] chose mostly appropriate topics for [his/her] goals. [S/he] attempted to create goals around important targets, which were designed to move the work forward when they were achieved. For the most part, [s/he] succeeded, although

(continued)

GOAL-ORIENTED AND DRIVE FOR RESULTS
Downloadable Form 6.9 *(Continued)*

the goals were not particularly innovative. Also, [s/he] set some goals around day-to-day or maintenance work that was already being easily achieved; these goals needed to be modified to encourage more of a drive to the attainment of significant results. For the most part, [   ] goals were easily communicated, although the language of some of them needed to be strengthened. As expected, they were set in conjunction with [his/her] manager and [his/her] view of what should be accomplished over the year.

[   ] understood that [s/he] was supposed to use the goals [s/he] set to guide [his/her] performance over the course of the year. [S/he] attempted to do this but would typically lose sight of these goals, only pulling them out again when prompted by [his/her] manager as part of a performance management conversation. [   ] drive for results and momentum tended to come more from what was the burning issue of the day than from the strategic goals [s/he] had previously set.

When [   ] revisited [his/her] goals, [s/he] used their specificity, measurability, and time lines to help plan and organize the work and resources for [his/her] projects. This attention to goals seemed temporary, however, and [   ] often struggled to maintain [his/her] eye on the end goal. [His/her] drive for results was strong but seemed to be focused on the results for that day, week, or crisis. [S/he] would rarely evaluate [his/her] progress against the goals [s/he] set at the beginning of the year and could not typically say where [s/he] was in terms of proximity to the long-term desired result. [S/he] was better at tackling obstacles to short- versus long-term goals if they were more of the short-term nature. If [s/he] found [him/herself] off track in pursuit of a larger goals, [s/he] was typically at a loss about how to get the overall plan back on track.

[   ] displayed a moderate sense of urgency to achieve the outcomes [s/he] established at the beginning of the year. This urgency tended to ebb and flow based on the pace and workload of the business, and again she did a better job driving for immediate versus long-term results. However, [s/he] was motivated to achieve all [his/her] targets and this incentive contributed to [him/her] achieving most of the goals [s/he] set. [S/he] did not, however, exceed any of these goals.

GOAL-ORIENTED AND DRIVE FOR RESULTS
Downloadable Form 6.9 *(Continued)*

Specific examples of when [ ] showed [s/he] was goal-oriented with a drive for results were:

_____

_____

_____

_____

_____

_____

Specific examples of when [ ] failed to show [s/he] was goal-oriented with a drive for results were:

_____

_____

_____

_____

_____

_____

Did Not Meet Expectations

Last year, [ ] did not meet expectations in being goal-oriented with a drive for results. [S/he] fell short in the areas of setting appropriate goals as well as driving to achieve them.

[ ] did not seem to understand the role of individual goal setting in terms of advancing large-scale performance or achieving large-scale success. [S/he] did not set goals that linked to the goals of the department or to the larger company. Instead, when [s/he] set goals at all (which [s/he] often did not), [s/he] paid no attention to anything but [his/her] own objectives.

[ ] struggled in the actual process of setting goals. All [his/her] goals had problems with one or more elements of the SMART formula: (1) They were not specific, but were vague statements of what [s/he] would try to do; (2) they were not measurable and included no quantitative targets; (3) they were not achievable, but instead were either impossible to achieve or extremely easy; (4) they were not relevant and had no relation to what the department or company was trying to

(continued)

GOAL-ORIENTED AND DRIVE FOR RESULTS
Downloadable Form 6.9 *(Continued)*

achieve; and (5) they were not time-bound and included no deadlines. [S/he] also did not set goals for all time periods; [s/he] crafted some long-term goals without any short-term objectives to lay out the road map on how to achieve them but also crafted numerous, random short-term goals, none of which linked to any long-range plans.

Most of [   ] goals were not set around significant targets. [S/he] set many goals around day-to-day or maintenance work that [s/he] was already readily achieving. [   ] showed no innovation in [his/her] goal setting. The wording of many of [his/her] goals was extremely convoluted and as such the goals were difficult to communicate. Many were also set without manager approval and had to be significantly readjusted throughout the year.

Once [   ] goals were set, [s/he] tended to forget them and did not use them as drivers in [his/her] attempt to obtain results. The results [s/he] wanted to achieve were not clearly outlined in the goals [s/he] did have, and this lack or confusion of goals frequently impeded momentum in achieving results, or where there was momentum, it often was directed in an inappropriate area.

The lack of specificity, measurability, and time lines of [   ] goals also hurt [his/her] ability to plan and organize the work and resources to have the best chance of achieving the desired results. [S/he] also had trouble evaluating [his/her] progress against these weak goals, which hurt [his/her] ability to get back on track when [s/he] went off course, which happened frequently.

In general, when [   ] did go off track in pursuit of [his/her] goals, [s/he] tended to give up quickly. [S/he] did not show any tenacity in tackling the barriers or obstacles to results [s/he] wanted to achieve. In other instances, [   ] hung on to a goal too long, even when it was clear that it was the wrong goal or that [s/he] would have to make some significant changes to it. This complete lack of or misdirected drive meant that [   ] was unable to achieve even the most basic goals.

Specific examples of when [   ] failed to show [s/he] was goal-oriented with a drive for results were:

_____

_____

_____

_____

_____

INITIATIVE*
Downloadable Form 6.10

Exceeded Expectations

Last year, [   ] exceeded expectations in the area of initiative. Others described [him/her] consistently with many phrases that indicate this skill, such as a "self-starter" or "go-getter" or someone with a "can do attitude."

[   ] required very little supervision in [his/her] work over the past year. When [s/he] was given a task, [s/he] would take in whatever directions were needed (even if they were vague) and then would be off and running on [his/her] own. [   ] was excellent at acting preventively, to try to avoid issues arising in [his/her] work. When problems arose, [s/he] would always take the initiative to figure out a solution on [his/her] own before running to someone else for help or to fix whatever it was. There were no instances where [   ] had to be prompted by someone else to complete a task or assignment.

This proactive approach had many positive results. It contributed to [   ] accomplishing all [his/her] goals set for the year, many in advance of the deadlines. When goals were met, or in fact when any work was completed, [   ] would show initiative by looking ahead to what could be done as the next step and take that on as well. This exploration of new opportunities and doing things without being told showed that [   ] displayed an overall pattern of seeking solutions and chances to "move the ball ahead."

[   ] was always eager and willing to take on new assignments or responsibilities. [S/he] certainly showed this was true when specifically asked to help with something, and [s/he] would also proactively ask colleagues if they needed any help. [S/he] was also not a procrastinator. When something needed to be done, [   ] would get right on it without delay. If extra effort was needed on a project, [   ] was always the first to volunteer to put in the extra time.

[   ] remained alert to any new opportunities or approaches that could improve a process, whether in [his/her] own work or in that of the broader team. [S/he] was always looking for feedback that would help gather this information, and if none was forthcoming, [s/he] would solicit it. The questions that [s/he] asked and information [s/he] learned through [his/her] initiative frequently served the broader good of the team. And it was clear that this team advancement and development was the motivation for [   ] initiative, not [his/her] own personal advancement.

(continued)

INITIATIVE
Downloadable Form 6.10 *(Continued)*

Specific examples of when [   ] showed exceptional initiative were:

_____

_____

_____

_____

_____

_____

_____

_____

_____

Met Expectations

[   ] met expectations in the area of initiative over the past year. [S/he] did not require much supervision, and there were instances where [s/he] went above and beyond in [his/her] actions.

[   ] did especially well meeting expectations around initiative in regard to [his/her] prescribed goals. When [   ] was given a specific project, [s/he] was able to take it and run with it, without procrastination or assistance. When questions arose, [s/he] did [his/her] best to get answers [him/herself] before running to someone else for help. Additionally, when problems arose, [s/he] tried to find solutions on [his/her] own and typically would find some options, although without [s/he] did not make the extra effort to see if the chosen solutions were the best ones or just the easiest, most available ones. Finally, when [   ] had to make a decision, [s/he] would not delay in taking action but would attempt to choose a path in a timely manner. [S/he] was usually, though not always, successful in this regard. In particular, there were times where [s/he] could have shown more initiative in prompting a group to come to a consensus on a course of action.

Where [   ] did less well on initiative was in attempting to exceed any of the stated goals. In general, once a goal was accomplished, [s/he] would need direction for the next task or project, rather than using anything learned on the past project as an idea for an advancement, improvement, or next step. In other words, [   ] initiative skills tended to operate within the bounds of assigned work

INITIATIVE
Downloadable Form 6.10 *(Continued)*

but not in any attempt to proactively advance to the next level of change or development.

[   ] frequently took the initiative to check in with [his/her] coworkers, to see if there was anything [s/he] could help with. Again, though, this initiative was confined to the comforts of the team. No initiative to reach out to other teams, groups, or organizations in search of possible synergies was made over the past year.

In general, [   ] displayed an adequate amount of initiative last year. [S/he] attempted to function independently and was successful in this regard on normal, daily tasks, although lacking in the expansion of this "can do" attitude to broader, more complex situations.

Specific examples of when [   ] showed initiative were:

_____

_____

_____

_____

_____

Specific examples of when [   ] failed to show initiative were:

_____

_____

_____

_____

_____

Did Not Meet Expectations

[   ] did not meet expectations in the area of initiative last year. [S/he] required constant supervision and seemed nearly incapable of acting on [his/her] own without explicit direction and approval.

Repeatedly, [   ] would be given a task and then either (1) procrastinate and choose not to begin it at all, or (2) complete the first, often miniscule part of the task, and then immediately return for feedback and/or more direction. There were also instances when [   ] had to make a decision but delayed until it was too late and a course was chosen for [him/her]. Actions such as these revealed [   ]

(continued)

INITIATIVE
Downloadable Form 6.10 *(Continued)*

tendency to act in the complete opposite way of someone showing initiative, and there were negative repercussions to [his/her] lack of action, such as lost deals, networking opportunities, etc.

[   ] showed a complete lack of interest in taking on new work beyond what was assigned. Regarding that current work, [s/he] displayed no interest in exploring other opportunities or approaches beyond the norm. There were no examples of [him/her] making suggestions to improve a process or of proactively taking steps to figure out what to do next once the current project was completed. The general sense was that [   ] relied on others to do the thinking for [him/her] in many aspects of work.

Not only did [   ] fail to show initiative on [his/her] regular tasks, but [s/he] also lacked initiative in dealing with any issues that arose. If a problem came up on one of [his/her] projects, [s/he] would immediately stop work and ask for help rather than attempting to figure out a solution on [his/her] own. Even if an unexpected situation arose that was not a problem, [   ] would not be able to generate or apply a new technique to deal with it but would again shut down work until getting help. If extra effort was needed on a project, [   ] never volunteered on [his/her] own to put in extra time but instead always had to be asked by [his/her] manager or coworkers.

This lack of initiative hampered [   ] ability to complete [his/her] goals in a timely manner. Many assignments did not get finished, and there were also no examples of [him/her] pitching in to help colleagues with any of their assignments. [S/he] definitely never took the lead in bringing any sort of improvement to the team or helping the group adapt to a change. Rather, [s/he] would hang back and rely on others to provide the sufficient prompting needed for [him/her] to adopt a new process or behavior.

Specific examples of when [   ] failed to show initiative were:

_____

_____

_____

_____

_____

_____

JOB AND INDUSTRY KNOWLEDGE*
Downloadable Form 6.11

Exceeded Expectations

[   ] exceeded expectations in the area of job and industry knowledge last year.

From the start of the year, [s/he] displayed a higher-than-average level of familiarity with the industry. [S/he] could, at any time, speak knowledgably about any aspect of the field. [S/he] could hold an educated discussion on topics such as the leaders in the field, recent or historical advances in the field, current competitors, or best practices. [S/he] could also describe in detail the general vision for the industry as well as converse about possible visions for the future.

Despite this high starting level of industry knowledge, [   ] was always working to gain more information about the field. [S/he] was often seen reading various trade publications or web sites and attended every industry-related session or workshop offered by the company. [S/he] enjoyed engaging colleagues in conversations about current happenings in the industry and even worked to organize small discussion groups or meetings about relevant industry topics. [S/he] also looked outside the company for inputs to these discussions, which [s/he] would often find in industry-based professional groups. [S/he] was a member of several of these groups and took on leadership roles as needed.

By fostering these resources, [   ] was always up-to-date about any changes in the industry. [S/he] made sure to let colleagues know about these changes immediately, whether they were changes to requirements, regulations, or other information. There were also several examples where [   ] was able to anticipate some industry changes that put [him/her] and the team in general ahead of the curve in adapting to these changes.

In addition to industry knowledge, [   ] knowledge about [his/her] job also exceeded expectations. [S/he] displayed complete understanding about all facets of [his/her] job. [S/he] was frequently referred to as an "expert," "master," or "authority" of job knowledge.

[His/her] job knowledge showed both breadth and depth: [s/he] showed a broad understanding of all aspects of the job and could also discuss with incredible detail any particular aspect. [S/he] showed extensive knowledge of the job's responsibilities, requirements, and resources. [S/he] knew all about the job's clients (internal and external) and competitors. [S/he] successfully applied

(continued)

JOB AND INDUSTRY KNOWLEDGE
Downloadable Form 6.11 *(Continued)*

[his/her] education and experience to the functional aspects of the job. This meant [s/he] was never at a loss where to start a task, what to do if problems arose, or what to do once a task was finished.

One of the best indicators of [   ] extensive level of job knowledge was that [s/he] served as the department's "encyclopedia." [s/he] constantly helped [his/her] coworkers with questions they had about their own job knowledge and always was willing to share any information [s/he] had.

Specific examples of when [   ] showed exceptional job and industry knowledge were:

_____

_____

_____

_____

_____

_____

_____

_____

Met Expectations

[   ] met expectations in the area of job and industry knowledge over the past year.

[S/he] displayed an average level of familiarity with the industry. [S/he] could speak knowledgeably on the basic aspects of the industry and could contribute at least a few points on topics such as the leaders in the field, recent or historical advances in the field, current competitors, or best practices. [S/he] did a better job at keeping up with current trends than at forecasting possible changes or advances in the industry's future.

[   ] made modest attempts to improve [his/her] industry knowledge over the year. [S/he] would read articles in trade journals or attend relevant professional or company-sponsored meetings, although typically only when others suggested these activities. [   ] was not proactive in searching out new, independent ways to improve [his/her] industry knowledge, nor did [s/he] take on any leadership roles in this regard.

JOB AND INDUSTRY KNOWLEDGE
Downloadable Form 6.11 *(Continued)*

When changes occurred in the industry, [   ] was open to adapting to them. [S/he] attempted to keep current on these changes, such as adjustments to or releases of new requirements, regulations, or processes. [S/he] would also pass on any new knowledge [s/he] gained to others, as needed.

[   ] possessed the level of job knowledge appropriate for [his/her] role, background, and experience. [S/he] knew the basics of key areas such as responsibilities, requirements, and resources. [S/he] did not go above and beyond in acquiring extra knowledge about clients or competitors, but again demonstrated that [s/he] was proficient with the basic facts. In terms of functional knowledge, [   ] typically had enough information to begin a variety of tasks but would often get stuck if unexpected problems arose and in those instances would have to turn to others for their expertise.

When [   ] was missing a key piece of job knowledge, [s/he] would attempt to educate [his/her]self on it and tried to maintain these learnings throughout the year. [S/he] accomplished this with varied success—for some tasks, [s/he] was able to incorporate new information quickly, while for others, [s/he] struggled with the knowledge and regularly had to ask for help or would make lots of errors if left on [his/her] own.

[   ] would not be regarded as an expert or master of job knowledge. However, [s/he] could be counted on to readily share the basic information [s/he] had with colleagues when asked.

Specific examples of when [   ] showed job and industry knowledge were:

_____

_____

_____

_____

Specific examples of when [   ] failed to show job and industry knowledge were:

_____

_____

_____

_____

(continued)

JOB AND INDUSTRY KNOWLEDGE
Downloadable Form 6.11 *(Continued)*

Did Not Meet Expectations

[   ] did not meet expectations in the area of job and industry knowledge last year.

From the start of the year, [s/he] displayed a lower-than-average level of familiarity with the industry. [S/he] could not speak knowledgeably about basic aspects of the field. [S/he] could not hold a discussion on topics such as the leaders in the field, recent or historical advances, current competitors, or best practices. [S/he] could not describe the general vision for the industry nor converse about possible visions for the future.

Over the course of the year, [   ] did not try to increase [his/her] knowledge about the industry. [S/he] did not subscribe to any trade publications nor seem to do reading of any kind about the field. [S/he] was not a member of any industry-based organizations and did not join any during the year. [   ] did not take advantage of any of the company-offered education events, and [s/he] was [s/he] never heard discussing general industry-related topics with [his/her] peers.

[   ] did not keep up-to-date on changes in the industry over the past year and certainly did not work to try to anticipate any of these changes. [S/he] did not attempt to keep current on adjustments to or releases of new regulations or processes and instead relied on others to bring [him/her] up to speed on anything [s/he] needed to know. [S/he] did not attempt to put any of her education or experience to work in trying to expand the information [s/he] had about the field.

[   ] also demonstrated a lower-than-average level of knowledge about [his/her] job. [His/her] job knowledge was significantly out-of-date and was not commensurate with [his/her] level of education and experience. Yet, [s/he] did nothing to improve this knowledge over the course of the year.

[   ] lack of job knowledge spanned several areas. To start with, [s/he] did not seem to have knowledge of the basic job responsibilities and requirements. [S/he] also failed to demonstrate a strong functional knowledge, which resulted in several instances of [him/her] not knowing where to start a task or what to do next after one task was finished. [   ] also seemed to lack the expected level of knowledge of resources or clients, either internal and external.

JOB AND INDUSTRY KNOWLEDGE
Downloadable Form 6.11 *(Continued)*

This lack of job knowledge meant that [   ] had to ask for help on almost every assignment. When [s/he] tried to work on [his/her] own, [s/he] had extensive errors in [his/her] work. Despite these incidents, [   ] did not try to improve [his/her] level of job knowledge, declining any offers of training, mentoring, coaching, or development on job-related topics.

[   ] was not viewed as an expert in any aspect of job or industry knowledge, and there were no observed examples of [   ] sharing [his/her] knowledge in either of these areas with colleagues or clients.

Specific examples of when [   ] failed to show job and industry knowledge were:

_____

_____

_____

_____

_____

_____

_____

_____

_____

_____

NEGOTIATING AND INFLUENCING*
Downloadable Form 6.12

Exceeded Expectations

Last year, [   ] exceeded expectations in the area of negotiating and influencing skills. [S/he] was a model of tact in all [his/her] dealings with other parties when [s/he] was trying to strike a deal or persuade them of a point of view.

In terms of negotiations, [   ] was largely successful due to [his/her] thorough preparation. [S/he] would spend significant time thinking about what [s/he] wanted out of the negotiations as well as what the other party cared about. This sincere desire to meet both parties' interests went a long way toward helping to broker an agreeable deal.

[   ] also showed a high level of creativity in coming up with options that would work for both sides. [S/he] did not get stuck in the "my way or the highway" competitive thinking that would sink many negotiations. The agreements that [   ] brokered often exceeded the goals both parties had coming in to the discussions. What was also extraordinary was that [s/he] was able to achieve success in both the smallest and the most complex (e.g., with multiple parties) deals.

[   ] understood the balance between obtaining substance and fostering relationships in negotiations and always strove to achieve both in any given deal. [S/he] consistently walked away from the bargaining table having achieved what [s/he] wanted but never at the expense of the working relationship with the other party. If conflict or misunderstandings occurred, [   ] would work to resolve them fairly, again by delicately balancing the ability to express [his/her] interests clearly while sincerely listening to those of the other party.

In the few instances where [   ] had to walk away from a deal because the parties could not agree, [s/he] made sure to leave the door open so negotiations could resume in the future with no ill will.

In more general examples of influence, [   ] displayed the same high level of tact and success. [S/he] was adept at swaying others to [his/her] way of thinking, largely because [s/he] could state [his/her] thoughts clearly and make a credible case. [S/he] always presented [his/her] ideas in a language that the other party could understand and buy into.

NEGOTIATING AND INFLUENCING
Downloadable Form 6.12 *(Continued)*

[   ] effective style of negotiating and influence helped [him/her] to achieve, and in fact surpass, [his/her] performance goals for the year and also helped the department significantly advance on its goals for the year.

Specific examples of when [   ] showed exceptional negotiating and influencing skills were:

_____

_____

_____

_____

_____

_____

_____

Met Expectations

[   ] met expectations in the area of negotiating and influencing skills over the past year. [S/he] was seen as an average negotiator, resulting in agreements that met but did not exceed stated goals. In more general persuasive situations, [s/he] influenced her audience on a regular but not consistent basis.

[   ] understood the framework for successful negotiations and was able to apply this framework. [S/he] prepared for formal negotiations and spent time both working to express [his/her] interests clearly as well as think of what those of the other party might be.

At the bargaining table, [   ] attempted to implement the negotiation plans [s/he] had made. Due to this planning, [s/he] typically reached a resolution with the other party. However, those agreements often stopped short of achieving all the goals of both sides. [His/her] main negotiation style was to compromise—give a little to get a little—which maintained the good feelings of all parties, but at the expense of a more inspired, collaborative agreement that met or exceeded all the goals of both parties.

When conflict arose during negotiations, [   ] attempted to resolve it and was mostly effective in this regard, although there were a few instances where the tension affected working relationships and [s/he] had to call in help to mend some associations.

(continued)

NEGOTIATING AND INFLUENCING
Downloadable Form 6.12 *(Continued)*

In terms of daily influencing situations, [   ] again met expectations. In a do-or-die situation, [s/he] typically could get the other party to come around to some type of consensus, but [his/her] methods of doing this (either being heavy-handed or pleading) were not always the most effective.

Specific examples of when [   ] showed strong negotiating and influencing skills were:

_____

_____

_____

_____

_____

_____

_____

_____

Specific examples of when [   ] failed to show strong negotiating and influencing skills were:

_____

_____

_____

_____

_____

_____

_____

_____

NEGOTIATING AND INFLUENCING
Downloadable Form 6.12 *(Continued)*

Did Not Meet Expectations

[   ] did not meet expectations in the area of negotiating and influencing skills last year. In repeated instances, [s/he] failed to successfully navigate situations where [s/he] was called on to influence another party or reach an agreement that was suitable to both parties.

In terms of formal negotiations, [   ] rarely prepared in advance of meetings, which resulted in [him/her] failing to clearly state [his/her] interests or have any idea of what the other party cared about getting out of the deal. This lack of preparation hurt [his/her] ability to brainstorm optimal solutions for both sides. Rather than attempt to come up with creative options that worked for all parties, [   ] would either give in too quickly to the other party's demands or dig in unreasonably to [his/her] position.

This ineffective negotiation style resulted in an unnecessary level of tension between the parties with whom [   ] attempted to reach an agreement. When this conflict arose, [   ] was not adept in defusing it, and as a result, misunderstandings grew and relationships were damaged. There were also times when negotiations that [   ] was involved in collapsed, and [s/he] could not bring people back to the table to resume discussions. Several parties have indicated that they would prefer not to have to negotiate with [   ] in the future.

This lack of tact also applied to more general situations when [   ] tried to influence another party. Last year, [s/he] had a largely unsuccessful track record in persuading another party to [his/her] views. This inability to advance [his/her] position was mainly due to [his/her] inability to get [his/her] points across in a way the other party could understand and see as valid. Instead, [   ] style was more of trying to make unreasonable requests and present them as demands, almost daring the other party to disagree.

When [   ] was given feedback on [his/her] style, [s/he] was not able to make the necessary adjustments, but rather did a complete 180 and acquiesced too readily to the other party's demands. This confused style of negotiation and general influencing was rarely successful and resulted in long-term damage to working relationships and achievement of both [his/her] and the department's goals.

(continued)

NEGOTIATING AND INFLUENCING

Downloadable Form 6.12 *(Continued)*

Specific examples of when [   ] failed to show strong negotiating and influencing skills were:

_____

_____

_____

_____

_____

_____

_____

_____

_____

_____

_____

ORGANIZATIONAL AWARENESS*
Downloadable Form 6.13

Exceeded Expectations

[   ] exceeded expectations in the area of organizational awareness last year. [S/he] had all the basics of organizational awareness covered, and above that, [s/he] worked to look beyond [his/her] immediate world to the company's broader needs and goals.

[   ] consistently demonstrated that [s/he] had all the organizational knowledge needed for [his/her] role and beyond. [S/he] showed that [s/he] had a sound understanding of the department's goals as well as how they fit within the overall organizational goals. [S/he] also could clearly articulate the organizational structure and capabilities and again, how [his/her] department, and in fact [his/her] own role, fit into that structure.

[   ] worked to always stay up-to-date on any organizational changes by taking advantage of any company communications that were offered, from attending meetings to reading newsletters, press releases, and so on. [S/he] would also seek out other sources for gaining organizational awareness, such as attending industry or professional meetings and reading articles in the outside press about the company. This high level of organizational curiosity meant that [   ] was a great person to go to for referrals. If [s/he] could not help a person immediately with their request, [s/he] could always point them in the right direction.

[S/he] used this company knowledge to move [his/her] projects forward successfully. As [s/he] knew the people behind how processes work, [s/he] also knew whom to ask and how to proceed if a workaround was needed. [   ] repeatedly demonstrated [s/he] knew the key decision makers and decision-making processes of the organization and how to work within both effectively.

[   ] worked hard not to get involved in corporate politics, yet at the same time, [s/he] was aware of how things worked in reality and how this reality could at times differ from what was on paper. [S/he] was adept at using this knowledge to make appropriate decisions, such as knowing who should be present in certain meetings, even if it was just for face-time reasons.

[   ] consistently kept a broader organizational perspective in mind as [s/he] completed all [his/her] work or worked on problems that arose. In taking actions, especially ones involving larger-scale change, [s/he] would consider the impact

(continued)

ORGANIZATIONAL AWARENESS
Downloadable Form 6.13 *(Continued)*

on the larger department or other parts of the company that could be affected. [S/he] also did her best to ensure information was shared in a timely manner with all necessary parties across the company. All these actions required having intricate knowledge of the organization, and it was this level of knowledge that [   ] displayed over the entire year.

Specific examples of when [   ] showed exceptional organizational awareness were:

_____

_____

_____

_____

Met Expectations

[   ] met expectations in the area of organizational awareness over the past year. [S/he] showed that [s/he] had knowledge of the structure of the organization and how [his/her] role and department fit into the bigger picture. [S/he] was also interested in how [his/her] goals fit in and advanced the organization's larger goals.

[   ] displayed an understanding of the capabilities of [his/her] department and how to work with other groups to move projects ahead. [S/he] attempted to keep these other groups in mind in setting goals or solving problems, and for the most part succeeded. This was also true for communication; she tried to think about who would need to be kept in the loop and on what, and for the most part made accurate decisions in this regard.

[   ] kept abreast of all of the organizational communications that came out (reading newsletters, press releases, etc. and attending company meetings). [S/he] did not, however, search beyond the standard information that was released to try to improve [his/her] company knowledge.

[S/he] tried to be a good person to go to for referrals, although [s/he] tended to be more successful when the questions asked or referrals requested fell within scope of the job. If [   ] could not readily find an answer within her organizational network, [s/he] would often be stumped and tell the person asking for help that [s/he] could not assist them.

[   ] at times misstepped with company politics. This took a couple of different forms, such as not knowing whom to involve in meetings or decision-making

processes or not being respectful of some of the established communication protocols. For the most part, [s/he] tried to learn from these mistakes, although there remained some more sophisticated levels of political maneuveuring that [s/he] was not able to master.

These missteps were indicative of the broader issue for [   ] around organizational awareness, which was a lack of consistently thinking at the bigger firm level versus only at [his/her] immediate needs or work. [S/he] did not always consider [his/her] actions from the point of view of the entire organization but would at times confine [his/her] awareness only to the smaller department. This narrower view impacted [his/her] ability to solve problems more quickly and come up with decisions gaining widescale acceptance.

Specific examples of when [   ] showed organizational awareness were:

_____

_____

_____

_____

_____

_____

_____

Specific examples of when [   ] failed to show organizational awareness were:

_____

_____

_____

_____

_____

_____

Did Not Meet Expectations

[   ] did not meet expectations in the area of organizational awareness last year. [S/he] was not aware of, nor did [s/he] show any interest in, how [his/her] work contributed to the department's or broader organization's goals. Beyond that,

(continued)

ORGANIZATIONAL AWARENESS
Downloadable Form 6.13 *(Continued)*

[s/he] also displayed only the most minimal knowledge of the structure and capabilities of different groups in the organization.

[   ] did not stay at all current on the critical issues to the organization, much less the day-to-day communications. [S/he] did not take the time to read any company communications that were circulated (e.g., newsletters, press releases) and frequently made up excuses to not attend any town hall type meetings.

This lack of organizational knowledge or curiosity hampered [   ] work in several ways. [S/he] did not know the key influences and decision-making processes of the organization, which resulted in [his/her] decisions either getting stuck on the table or being derailed soon after because [s/he] did not obtain buy-in from other groups.

Additionally, [   ] did not take a broader organizational view when solving problems. This meant that again, the solutions [s/he] developed would often serve only as Band-Aids to the problem, and the issue would quickly rise again because [s/he] did not run the proposed solutions past affected groups.

[   ] made no effort to understand the politics at work behind some of some of the organizational relationships. [S/he] could not recognize which issues were worth pushing for versus when it was time to compromise. [S/he] also frequently failed to include the right people in meetings, decisions, or communications.

[   ] was not known as a go-to person within the company. Instead, [s/he] was frequently the person asking for help or referrals for different questions. This was true even for items that [s/he] asked about repeatedly and should have long since known the answers for.

The overall picture of [   ] organizational knowledge over the past year was one of a person with [his/her] head constantly down—focusing only on [his/her] own work, problems, issues and needs—rather than looking around and considering how [s/he] could and should interact with the broader company world, a synergy that would benefit the broader organization.

Specific examples of when [   ] failed to show organizational awareness were:

_____

_____

_____

_____

PRODUCTIVITY*
Downloadable Form 6.14

Exceeded Expectations

Last year, [   ] exceeded expectations in the area of productivity. [S/he] not only met but exceeded all production goals set for [him/her], and this exceptional productivity applied for both quantitative and qualitative goals.

[   ] maintained a level of peak performance on a consistent basis. In addition, when called for, [s/he] could take this high level of performance to an even higher level, operating on all cylinders for whatever time was needed to meet the goal, solve the problem, or avert the crisis. This often required expending extra energy, working extremely quickly, and putting in additional hours, all of which [   ] did with unflagging enthusiasm.

There were no instances over the course of the year when [   ] did not complete a production goal. Rather, [s/he] would meet those goals and continue to perform, either obtaining better results than expected or moving on to help colleagues meet their goals. Even at the times when [   ] was the most swamped, [s/he] was able to stay focused and meet or exceed the target of the work. As such, [   ] became the go-to person on the team; If something needed to get done and get done well, [   ] was always asked to contribute, no matter how swamped [s/he] already was with [his/her] own work.

This high level in productivity meant that [   ] made a substantial contribution to the success and growth of the team, and by association, the organization. [   ] produced abundant, measurable results on a consistent basis with no expectation that this productivity would flag in the future. Rather, [   ] has set the bar high on the level of expected productivity for the team, and numerous team members have indicated that they strive for that benchmark with their productions.

Specific examples of when [   ] showed exceptional productivity were:

_____

_____

_____

_____

_____

(continued)

PRODUCTIVITY
Downloadable Form 6.14 *(Continued)*

Met Expectations

[   ] met expectations in the area of productivity over the past year. [S/he] met all production goals set for [him/her], including those measured both quantitatively and qualitatively. In regard to production, [   ] would be considered a solid but not exceptional performer.

[   ] applied an average level of energy to her work. [S/he] would sometimes procrastinate the starting of a task but never so much that it would put [him/her] at risk of achieving the goal. Once starting the work, [   ] would do what was necessary to get the job done, but nothing more. There were few to no examples of when [s/he] expended extra energy to fine-tune [his/her] work or take it to the next level. As such, the goals were indeed achieved but without any added inspiration carried over to the next task or to colleagues with whom [s/he] worked.

When needed, [   ] could be asked to work faster to increase production based on an expressed need. However, as soon as that need ended, [   ] would revert to [his/her] same slower pace and energy level and settle for an average level of achievement, rather than looking for ways to continue to be inspired to produce more.

[   ] contributed to the work of the team in meeting the goals. However, these contributions were solely based on delivering what was asked for and nothing more. Rarely, if ever, did [   ] exceed normal standards of production.

Specific examples of when [   ] showed expected productivity were:

_____

_____

_____

_____

_____

Specific examples of when [   ] failed to show expected productivity were:

_____

_____

_____

_____

PRODUCTIVITY
Downloadable Form 6.14 *(Continued)*

Did Not Meet Expectations

[   ] did not meet expectations in the area of productivity. [S/he] fell below all or almost all production goals set last year, and this failure rate continued despite feedback and attempts at coaching. This diminished productivity occurred both for work that had quantitative measures and for projects measured more qualitatively.

The rate at which [   ] performed [his/her] work was consistently slower than was called for, and the output of [his/her] work suffered proportionally. There were no occasions when [s/he] produced more than what was expected; conversely, time after time, work had to be returned for additions or corrections to make it acceptable in line with the original goals.

[   ] poor production affected the overall production success of the group. [S/he] did not make any substantial contributions to the growth of the team or department. Instead, [his/her] colleagues frequently had to pitch in to cover work that [   ] had not been able to complete correctly or at all.

In general, [   ] did not display a high level of energy toward [his/her] work. If energy was expended, it was not done in an efficient manner. Any bursts of energy quickly petered out, and the overall trend for the year was that of minimal productivity.

Specific examples of when [   ] failed to show expected productivity were:

_____

_____

_____

_____

_____

_____

_____

PROFESSIONALISM*
Downloadable Form 6.15

Exceeded Expectations

[   ] exceeded expectations in the area of professionalism last year. [S/he] was the pinnacle of maturity, tact, and professional appearance and demeanor.

Regardless of the situation, [   ] exhibited strong emotional control. [S/he] cared deeply about [his/her] work but never let strong emotions take over a situation. Rather, [s/he] communicated [his/her] passion clearly and rationally. When faced with conflict or confrontations, [   ] displayed mature, appropriate reactions and strong self-control. [S/he] never "flew off the handle" or raised [his/her] voice at others. When faced with disappointment, [s/he] did not whine, complain, or overreact but rather would immediately recover and attempt to change the unfortunate circumstance.

[   ] was also a model of tact and diplomacy. [S/he] was frequently described as polished and professional by clients and colleagues alike. [S/he] displayed consistent poise in [his/her] work environment and handled all situations in a calm, objective manner. [   ] was sincere in [his/her] interactions with people. [S/he] always followed department and company protocol and was the model other coworkers attempted to follow in terms of paving relationships with new employees, difficult clients, or unknown visitors. [S/he] was always cordial and polite.

As a rule, [   ] worked to avoid unnecessary arguments. However, when they occurred, [s/he] maintained [his/her] tact, even in the face of the difficult, awkward, or conflicting situation. In these instances, [s/he] would keep [his/her] cool, navigate the sensitive situation with confidence and handle the issue constructively, ultimately achieving a resolution satisfactory to all parties. [His/her] communications in these examples were overwhelmingly honest, sincere, and diplomatic. Most importantly, [s/he] was able to do this and maintain healthy working relationships, ensuring that all groups would continue to want to collaborate in the future. [   ] was tactful both in delivering feedback to others as well as accepting criticism [him/her]self.

[   ] demonstrated the highest level of professional etiquette. There were no situations when [s/he] felt out of place, when [s/he] acted inappropriately, or when [his/her] behavior made another party feel uncomfortable. [S/he] was comfortable in any setting and successfully adapted [his/her] behavior to the tone of the meeting and/or clients. [   ] always showed impeccable dress and grooming.

PROFESSIONALISM
Downloadable Form 6.15 *(Continued)*

Through [his/her] professional demeanor, [s/he] represented the company extremely well and portrayed not only a positive first impression but maintained a positive impression through [his/her] appearance and actions. [   ] displayed this professional pride in everything [s/he] did—not just visually, but in [his/her] writing, [his/her] quest for continuous knowledge and improvement, and in [his/her] consistently strong professional values.

Specific examples of when [   ] showed exceptional professionalism were:

_____

_____

_____

_____

_____

Met Expectations

[   ] met expectations in the area of professionalism over the past year. Specifically [s/he] met expectations in the areas of maturity, tact, and professional appearance and demeanor.

In most instances, [   ] exhibited control over [his/her] emotions. [S/he] cared about [his/her] work but tried to never let strong emotions take over a situation. Rather, [s/he] communicated rationally, although at times, [his/her] passion about something would compromise the clarity of the message. When faced with conflict or confrontations, [   ] generally displayed mature, appropriate reactions and strong self-control. However, there were a few times when [s/he] flew off the handle and raised [his/her] voice at others. In these situations, [   ] knew [s/he] had acted inappropriately, and when [his/her] emotions calmed down, [s/he] apologized and attempted to rebuild the relationship. When faced with disappointment, [s/he] tried to see the bigger picture and focus on changing the circumstance, although typically [s/he] could not do this without first whining or complaining about how the situation was unfair.

[   ] strove to exhibit tact and diplomacy. At times, [s/he] was described as polished and professional by clients and colleagues alike. [S/he] tried to display consistent poise in [his/her] work environment and handle situations in a calm, objective manner. [S/he] also strove for sincerity in [his/her] interactions with

(continued)

people. [   ] did a better job at being tactful in easy situations or when [s/he] focused on this skill. The tactfulness suffered somewhat when situations got tense. If [s/he] didn't remain mindful of remaining poised, [his/her] instincts were less diplomatic. [   ] attempted to follow department and company protocol, although at times did not seem aware of what the protocol was (or chose to disregard it).

[   ] tried to avoid unnecessary arguments. [S/he] recognized the need for maintaining [his/her] tact, even in the face of a difficult, awkward, or conflicting situation. [S/he] was typically successful although not stellar in these efforts, in particular struggling if something pushed one of [his/her] hot buttons. In these instances, [s/he] failed to keep [his/her] cool or handle the issue constructively. When this happened, it was impossible to achieve a resolution satisfactory to all parties without bringing in another party to mediate. In general, [his/her] communication style was perceived as honest, sincere, and diplomatic. [S/he] was able to maintain healthy working relationships with most clients and coworkers, and most groups reported wanting to collaborate with [him/her] in the future, although, again, some of these relationships had to be smoothed over to obtain this result. [   ] showed an average level of tact both in delivering feedback to others as well as accepting criticism [him/her]self.

[   ] demonstrated a satisfactory level of professional etiquette. In most situations, [his/her] professional behavior was appropriate; however there were a few situations where [s/he] felt out of place, where [s/he] acted slightly inappropriately or when [his/her] behavior made another party feel uncomfortable. [S/he] was at ease in most settings, although it was difficult for [him/her] to adapt [his/her] behavior if the tone of the meeting and/or clients was different from [his/her] instincts or what [s/he] expected. [   ] showed appropriate dress and grooming. Through [his/her] professional demeanor, [s/he] represented the company adequately. [S/he] portrayed a neutral to positive first impression and maintained this impression through [his/her] appearance and actions. [   ] displayed an average level of professional pride in other areas besides visually: [S/he] had moderate success in writing professionally, [s/he] had a modest interest in continuous knowledge and improvement, and [s/he] did not have any discordant professional values.

PROFESSIONALISM
Downloadable Form 6.15 *(Continued)*

Specific examples of when [   ] showed professionalism were:

_____

_____

_____

_____

Specific examples of when [   ] failed to show professionalism were:

_____

_____

_____

_____

Did Not Meet Expectations

[   ] did not meet expectations in the area of professionalism last year. [S/he] fell short in the areas of maturity, tact, and professional appearance and demeanor.

[   ] had difficulty maintaining control on [his/her] emotions. [S/he] often let [his/her] strong emotions take over a situation. Even if [s/he] was right about a point, [s/he] often let [his/her] overzealous passion about the topic compromise her ability to communicate clearly and rationally. This became even more of an issue when [   ] was faced with conflict or confrontations. In these instances, [   ] displayed immature, inappropriate reactions and a complete lack of self-control. [S/he] frequently flew off the handle and could often be heard raising [his/her] voice at others. When faced with disappointment, [   ] typical response was to whine, complain, or overreact rather than attempt to engage in a productive activity to change the unfortunate circumstance. [   ] continued these inappropriate emotional reactions throughout the year, even after given specific, targeted feedback on how to adjust them to gain more self-control.

[   ] also had problems exhibiting tact and diplomacy. [S/he] was frequently described as unpolished and unprofessional by clients and colleagues alike. [S/he] rarely exhibited poise in [his/her] work environment and, as noted, reacted to most situations in an emotional rather than a calm, objective manner. [S/he] often deviated from department and company protocol in [his/her] actions. [S/he]

(continued)

struggled in situations where [s/he] had to build or maintain sensitive relationships with parties such as new employees, difficult clients, or unknown visitors. Many of these groups reported that [s/he] was brusque or impolite.

Over the year, [   ] engaged in numerous unnecessary arguments. In fact, any difficult, awkward, or conflicting situation that [s/he] was involved in seemed to end in harsh words. [   ] seemed unable to keep [his/her] cool, navigate a sensitive situation with confidence, or handle the issue constructively. This resulted in not being able to achieve a resolution satisfactory to all parties, without having someone else brought in to mediate. [   ] communications in these examples, were perceived as insincere, incendiary, and undiplomatic. [His/her] lack of tact severely hurt [his/her] ability to maintain healthy working relationships, and in fact many groups, if given the option, chose not to collaborate with [   ] in future dealings. [   ] was equally unsuccessful at tactfully delivering feedback to others as [s/he] was at gracefully accepting criticism.

[   ] demonstrated low levels of professional etiquette. There were many situations when [s/he] appeared out of place, when [s/he] acted inappropriately, or when [his/her] behavior made another party feel uncomfortable. [S/he] was uncomfortable in many professional settings and could not adapt [his/her] behavior to the tone of the meeting and/or clients. [   ] consistently had issues with [his/her] professional dress and grooming. There were several instances where [s/he] had to be given feedback or told to adjust [his/her] appearance to make it more appropriate. [His/her] professional demeanor failed to represent the company well. [S/he] often portrayed a negative first impression. [   ] failed to display a professional pride in anything [s/he] did. [S/he] struggled in [his/her] professionalism, and this struggle was portrayed not just visually, but in [his/her] sloppy writing, [his/her] lack of desire for improvement, and [his/her] questionable professional values.

Specific examples of when [   ] failed to show professionalism were:

_____

_____

_____

_____

_____

_____

QUALITY*

Downloadable Form 6.16

Exceeded Expectations

Last year, [   ] exceeded expectations in [his/her] quality of work. [S/he] consistently produced work of the highest value and was fully committed to excellence in everything [s/he] did.

In any type or size of project or task, [   ] demonstrated an unflagging commitment to accuracy and thoroughness. This commitment meant that [his/her] work was consistently delivered without errors. This zero-tolerance-for-error standard was a personal benchmark that [   ] held [him/herself] to, and [s/he] would take special steps or precautions to make sure all deliverables were mistake-free. [S/he] excelled in detecting mistakes or flaws in tasks or processes and would not rest until the imperfection was resolved.

Beyond [his/her] own work, [   ] also assisted other team members with the quality of their work. [S/he] was always willing to proofread or check any of [his/her] colleagues' work, as [s/he] was dedicated to the quality of the work coming out of the department as a whole. As such, other employees used [   ] work as a model for quality and strove to get theirs up to the same high level.

Even when producing the highest quality of work, [   ] would not ease up on [his/her] standards but would look to see how [s/he] could improve a process to produce even higher quality. This ongoing quest for state-of-the-art perfection showed that [   ] recognized the competitive edge gained through continuous work of the highest quality, and [s/he] was never satisfied with or proud of anything less.

What set [   ] quality of work apart was, more than anything, its consistency. The unflagging accuracy and highest levels of excellence were seen in work as small as a two-line e-mail and as large as a formal project report or high-level presentation to a large group.

Specific examples of when [   ] work showed exceptional quality were:

_____

_____

_____

(continued)

Met Expectations

[   ] met expectations in the area of quality of work over the past year. Wherever the standards of quality were, [s/he] typically hit them right on the nose rather than going above or falling below this benchmark.

[   ] understood the relationship of high-quality work to the overall success of the department. As such, [s/he] strove to produce work of the highest value. [S/he] spent time trying to deliver work that was error-free by engaging in activities such as proofreading and fact checking. For the most part, these activities were successful, and [   ] deliverables were largely error-free. At times, however, accuracy was not 100%. The thoroughness of detecting mistakes seemed to suffer in times when [s/he] had to multitask, when the task was extremely complex or, conversely, when it was seen as a throwaway task that, in [   ] mind, did not call for the same standard of quality.

For the most part, [   ] was willing to help colleagues achieve high levels of quality in their work as well. [S/he] definitely recognized the need to work together to attain the highest quality. Again, though, these collaborations suffered a bit when [   ] got wrapped up in [his/her] own tasks.

[   ] displayed pride in [his/her] work and showed sincere concern for its quality. The work [s/he] produced over the past year was largely of acceptable quality, albeit with a few exceptions.

Specific examples of when [   ] work showed high quality were:

_____

_____

_____

_____

Specific examples of when [   ] work failed to show high quality were:

_____

_____

_____

_____

Did Not Meet Expectations

[   ] did not meet expectations in the quality of [his/her] work last year. [S/he] was aware of the quality standards but consistently fell short of those standards on a wide variety of tasks. [His/her] work was considered by numerous parties, both internal and external to the group, to be well below par.

[   ] seemed to display an extremely cavalier attitude toward accuracy, viewing it more as a "nice to have" than as a "need to have." [S/he] would frequently submit work riddled with mistakes and did not improve this error rate even after feedback or coaching. [S/he] stated that [s/he] thought as long as people got the gist of the message, that errors did not matter, and so [s/he] did not see value in spending time trying to catch them. [   ] applied this standard to everything from e-mails, which would be riddled with typos, to spreadsheets, which often contained numerous calculation mistakes.

[S/he] did not spend time proofreading work before submitting it. [S/he] would not ask colleagues to help [him/her] improve the quality of [his/her] work and was not relied on to help colleagues by reviewing their work. This lack of attention and collaboration resulted in slower outputs from the group as a whole than would otherwise be experienced with all parties pulling together to produce the highest quality.

[   ] did not recognize the relationship between high quality of work and the success of the department. Even when [s/he] worked on the most important deliverable of the year, the quality was still below where it needed to be and required others to contribute their efforts to get the work up to par. And even when [   ] was told to focus on a project and not submit it until it was the highest quality work possible, the quality was still below acceptable. Quality of work was not a priority to [   ], as shown consistently over the course of the year.

Specific examples of when [   ] work failed to show expected quality were:

_____

_____

_____

_____

SELF-DEVELOPMENT*
Downloadable Form 6.17

Exceeded Expectations

[   ] exceeded expectations in the area of self-development last year. [S/he] displayed an extremely high level of awareness of many aspects of [his/her] work including [his/her] strengths and areas for improvement. [S/he] also made extensive efforts to translate this awareness into positive behavior change, by leveraging [his/her] strengths and working to change [his/her] weaknesses.

In terms of general industry knowledge, [   ] displayed extraordinary curiosity about the goings on in [his/her] field, department, and specific role. [S/he] constantly attempted to expand [his/her] knowledge of the current trends in the industry by tapping into various sources such as trade journals, professional seminars, and conferences. Through these and other sources, [s/he] stayed abreast of best practices. Whenever [s/he] would find a gap in [his/her] understanding about something (e.g., products, technologies, resources, or advances in the field), [s/he] worked to fill these gaps through proactive learning. Due to these efforts, [s/he] was extremely up-to-date on current practices in the field.

[   ] was equally proactive in working to improve [his/her] own work behavior, both in pure job knowledge areas as well as in general, professional skills. [S/he] constantly evaluated [his/her] performance and used these assessments to set appropriate goals for further developing strengths and addressing areas of improvement. Once development goals were set, [   ] took the necessary initiative to make sure they were met, again tapping into myriad resources. [S/he] was equally proficient in all types of learning methods, from classroom to on-the-job training and all types of self-study. [S/he] also tapped into mentoring relationships in the company and used these relationships to help reach [his/her] development goals.

[   ] not only evaluated [his/her] own performance but also sought feedback from external sources, such as colleagues and clients. As they offered suggestions, [   ] quickly translated them into action with the constant goal of development. Once one goal was attained, [s/he] made sure to register the lessons learned from the past experience and then would quickly move on to take on another challenging assignment, with the goal of constant learning and development. These efforts made [   ] an expert both in her role and in the industry in general.

SELF-DEVELOPMENT
Downloadable Form 6.17 *(Continued)*

[   ] not only demonstrated that [s/he] had an active plan for [his/her] future career development; [s/he] also showed an exceptional interest in assisting in the development of others on the team. [His/her] philosophy was to create an atmosphere of ongoing learning in the department. To foster this, [s/he] constantly encouraged others to strive for continuous development and used [his/her] experience and resources to help them take advantage of their strengths and address any improvement areas.

Specific examples of when [   ] showed exceptional self-development were:

_____

_____

_____

_____

_____

_____

_____

_____

Met Expectations

[   ] met expectations in the area of self-development over the past year.

[S/he] worked to stay up-to-date about the main current trends in the industry by sampling resources including some trade journals or meetings. For the most part, these learnings would be driven by a need [   ] had in [his/her] work, rather than mere curiosity to learn more about the field.

[   ] showed an average amount of concern for [his/her] self-improvement. [S/he] seemed aware of [his/her] main areas of strengths and development needs. This awareness came mostly from feedback provided as part of the formal performance management process. For example, [s/he] worked to follow the development plan put in place to address the development areas laid out in the performance review. To do this, [s/he] relied mostly on standard resources, such as classroom training.

There was not a lot of evidence that [   ] took the initiative to invest in [his/her] development beyond these scripted goals and plans. [S/he] did not ask other

(continued)

SELF-DEVELOPMENT
Downloadable Form 6.17 *(Continued)*

parties, such as clients or colleagues, for feedback on [his/her] performance. Nor was [s/he] proactive in finding other opportunities to improve skills or knowledge beyond what was initially discussed for performance goals. [S/he] showed interest in getting a mentor in the company but did not follow up on this desire, and in fact this pattern occurred with several of [   ] development ideas throughout the year: A desire was expressed to improve some behavior but then follow-through evaporated as other "more important" (in [   ] view) activities took its place.

[   ] did a better job on self-development when [s/he] addressed a specific weakness. In these examples, [s/he] was very motivated to improve and asked for the appropriate amount of feedback during this process. Once these improvements were made, [s/he] was able to build off them with future improvements.

Overall, [   ] showed initiative to improve [his/her] job performance and content knowledge over the past year. [S/he] did not seem internally motivated to become an expert in the work he/she was responsible for, but [s/he] did try to achieve the development goals established as part of [his/her] formal career plan. Finally, [s/he] also showed interest in assisting in the development of others (although only when specifically asked) and was open to, although not a leader in, creating an atmosphere of continuous learning in the group.

Specific examples of when [   ] showed self-development were:

_____

_____

_____

_____

_____

_____

Specific examples of when [   ] failed to show self-development were:

_____

_____

_____

_____

_____

_____

Did Not Meet Expectations

[   ] did not meet expectations in the area of self-development last year. [S/he] did not display a high level awareness of many aspects of [his/her] work including a lack of awareness about [his/her] strengths or areas for improvement. Where there was an awareness of a lack of knowledge or development need, [s/he] did not make a significant attempt to address it.

[   ] did not display curiosity about [his/her] department or function. [S/he] never attempted to expand [his/her] knowledge of the current trends in the industry by tapping into various sources such as trade journals, professional seminars, etc., nor did [s/he] stay abreast of best practices. Where there were gaps in [his/her] understanding about products, technologies, resources or advances in the field, [s/he] was not motivated to fill these gaps through learning. [S/he] would not be considered up-to-date on current practices in the field.

In terms of [   ] own work behavior, [s/he] made few to no attempts to evaluate [his/her] performance and use that evaluation to set appropriate goals for leveraging strengths and tackling areas of improvement. [S/he] did not seek performance feedback from any external sources, relying only on manager-given feedback. [S/he] had no desire to foster a mentoring relationship (either upward or downward) in the company. If others offered suggestions for improvement, [   ] would typically ignore their suggestions. There were no instances where [   ] independently looked for opportunities to develop [him/herself], and this applied both for pure job knowledge areas and for general, professional skills. [S/he] did not appear to profit from any past experience [s/he] had in the field or the job.

Even when [   ] received specific feedback that [s/he] needed to focus on developing a certain area of [his/her] performance, the results of these efforts were tepid at best. [S/he] did not look for training or learning activities beyond the most basic resources. [S/he] resisted attending any training workshops or conferences, except in the few instances where these opportunities gave [him/her] some sort of side benefit (e.g., travel, time out of the office, getting out of other work, etc.). [S/he] did not look for opportunities to engage in on-the-job training by partnering with and learning from others, nor did [s/he] attempt address performance or knowledge gaps through self-study.

(continued)

SELF-DEVELOPMENT
Downloadable Form 6.17 *(Continued)*

Overall, [   ] put in only the most cursory efforts to improve [his/her] job performance or content knowledge over the past year. [S/he] seemed to have no motivation to get feedback on [his/her] behavior, nor to become any sort of expert in the work [s/he] does. [S/he] seemed to have no plan for [his/her] future career development and no desire to create one. Finally, [s/he] also showed no interest in assisting in the development of others or to help facilitate an atmosphere conducive to continuous learning in the group.

Specific examples of when [   ] failed to show self-development were:

_____

_____

_____

_____

_____

_____

_____

_____

_____

TEAMWORK*
Downloadable Form 6.18

Exceeded Expectations

[   ] exceeded expectations in the area of teamwork last year. [S/he] set the standard for being an effective team player, and [his/her] success in this area contributed to the broader success of [his/her] teams. In fact, that is how [   ] viewed success—as a win for the company and the team, rather than as a win for [him/herself].

[   ] displayed exceptional ease working with colleagues at all levels and in all roles. [S/he] displayed equal finesse in the role of a teacher—always looking to help coworkers; and learner— always open to hearing and understanding what coworkers had to say. Even when working on individual tasks, [   ] kept other people in mind and would not sacrifice their needs or goals for the sake of individual achievement.

[   ] was an outstanding member of any team he/she was on. [S/he] always met [his/her] own team goals on time and with high quality, thus showing exceptional accountability to the broader goals. [   ] consistently contributed ideas and skills toward the achievement of the common team goal and would proactively help other team members to do the same. [   ] was the consistent go-to person on the team if someone needed help, because [s/he] would either help the person or find someone else who could.

[   ] also displayed exceptional skill as a team leader. [S/he] navigated the team through all phases of team development, resulting in a high-performing team. [S/he] capitalized on the strengths and motivations of each team member and also invested significant time in cross-training for all members. In repeated examples, [   ] led the team through a consensus-building process that resulted in effective decisions that were supported by all members. [S/he] celebrated team successes frequently and made sure to share in and work through any failures. [S/he] often looked for ways to take part in or organize events to encourage team building. When conflicts occurred between team members, [   ] worked to resolve them quickly, fairly, and effectively. These resolutions were so effective that they brought the team closer together and set it up for further success, instead of creating lasting scars that would hamper future performance.

[   ] managed team resources well. [S/he] looked beyond [his/her] current teams to seek out synergies with other teams. This occurred both in a sharing of

(continued)

resources as well as in a sharing of ideas. These broader collaborations reinforced the sense of community and collaboration at all levels of the organization.

An important part of [   ] success in teamwork was [his/her] ability to value diversity in many ways. [S/he] consistently respected diversity in all its forms, from diversity of ideas and styles to cultures and backgrounds. And beyond simply respecting diversity, [   ] would seek out diversity among team members. [S/he] would actively try to include different groups, believing that having different perspectives from team members contributed to more effective teams.

Specific examples of when [   ] showed exceptional teamwork were:

_____

_____

_____

_____

_____

_____

_____

_____

Met Expectations

[   ] met expectations in the area of teamwork over the past year. [   ] understood that team success was a function of the success of all of its members. [S/he] was a solid team player who met the individual team goals assigned to [him/her], thus contributing to the achievement of the team's common goals.

[   ] attempted to build relationships with the other members, based on a sincere desire for team success. As a team member, [s/he] tried to remain open to input and ideas from other team members. There were a few instances where [s/he] put his own goals or successes ahead of what was best for the team. For the most part, however, [   ] showed a desire to collaborate and to work as a team to make decisions and solve problems. [S/he] accepted results from the consensus-building process.

TEAMWORK
Downloadable Form 6.18 *(Continued)*

[   ] was not overly territorial about [his/her] work. [S/he] seemed open to feedback from other team members and was also willing to pitch in and help others, although this occurred only when specifically asked. [S/he] was not proactive in looking for ways to help the team function more efficiently.

As a team leader, [   ] attempted to organize the team to best leverage the skills of all members. [S/he] displayed solid success as a leader when all parts of the team were functioning well; in these instances [   ] was effective in performing activities such as soliciting ideas from all members, securing resources, and celebrating team successes. [His/her] team leadership skills were compromised when discord occurred on the team. In these instances, [   ] tended to default to [his/her] ideas rather than being able to lead the team through a resolution process on a difficult decision where everyone felt their voice was heard or to effectively manage conflict among team members.

[   ] successes as a team leader were limited to [his/her] immediate teams. [S/he] did not tend to look beyond these teams for broader synergies that could created through links with other teams in the organization.

For the most part, [   ] valued diversity as an important component of team success. [S/he] was respectful of people with different ideas, styles, and backgrounds and understood how capitalizing on these differences result in a broader level of team success. Over the past year, there were no instances where [   ] acted inappropriately to colleagues different from [him/herself]. The one piece of valuing diversity on a team that [   ] did not display was an ability to champion diversity beyond what was naturally presented. In other words, if differences were currently present, [s/he] accepted them but [s/he] did not go out of [his/her] way to actively seek diverse backgrounds or points of view.

Specific examples of when [   ] showed teamwork were:

_____

_____

_____

_____

_____

(continued)

TEAMWORK
Downloadable Form 6.18 *(Continued)*

Specific examples of when [   ] failed to show teamwork were:

_____

_____

_____

_____

_____

Did Not Meet Expectations

[   ] did not meet expectations in the area of teamwork last year. [S/he] was not viewed as a team player and in almost any situation seemed motivated more by the achievement of [his/her] own personal agenda than by any broader, common team goal.

In general, [   ] did not work to develop significant relationships with other coworkers. [His/her] skills in cooperation and sharing seemed to be severely lacking. [   ] did not often consider others in his actions or decisions and neither looked to teach nor learn from others.

As a team member, [   ] failed to achieve [his/her] goals, and in fact on several occasions, actively worked against the larger team goals. [S/he] very rarely worked with other team members in an attempt to achieve consensus on team decisions, and [his/her] role in addressing issues that faced the team was typically one of a road blocker rather than problem solver. [   ] seemed overly willing to take credit for the team's successes, but refused to share in the failures, choosing instead to place blame on the performance of other team members. On numerous occasions, [   ] team members complained about [his/her] performance on the team, citing, among other things, a lack of respect for the ideas of other members, a territorial attitude to [his/her] work, and an unwillingness to collaborate on any but the most basic team goals. These failings in teamwork were significant enough to actually impede the year's success of the team.

As a team leader, [   ] was equally unsuccessful in displaying expected teamwork skills. [S/he] failed to complete the basics of team leadership, such as establishing roles and procedures. [   ] was unable to pull out the skills of various team members and organize the team to leverage these skills. In fact, team organization in general was almost entirely missing. [S/he] was also unable to successfully resolve conflicts among team members in an effective or timely manner, choosing to either ignore the issue or address it with unhelpful harshness.

TEAMWORK
Downloadable Form 6.18 *(Continued)*

[   ] did not display an ability to work collaboratively with members of other teams and was also unsuccessful in updating the necessary parties about [his/her] team's progress on various projects. [S/he] rarely, if ever, reached out to other teams to build synergy between their related goals.

Finally, [   ] also showed an inability to value the diversity that, in any setting, is crucial to establishing a successful team. [S/he] did not value diverse opinions put forth by team members and instead showed a level of disdain for any ideas that did not fit in with [his/her] current thinking. [S/he] never sought out ideas from any diverse groups and did not agree with the thinking that different styles contribute to a team's success. Additionally, [   ] displayed a lack of sensitivity in dealing with cultural and other background differences within the team and in fact in the wider environment. [S/he] treated diversity as a barrier to team success rather than a value to be fostered.

Specific examples of when [   ] failed to show teamwork were:

_____

_____

_____

_____

_____

_____

_____

_____

_____

_____

TECHNICAL SKILLS*
Downloadable Form 6.19

Exceeded Expectations

[   ] exceeded expectations in the area of technical skills last year. [S/he] consistently demonstrated a strong understanding of the current technical requirements of the job and then went beyond this level of understanding to constantly attempt to improve [his/her] skills through training, reading, self-study, and more.

[S/he] kept up-to-date on the technology aspects of the job and demonstrated great technical resourcefulness. [   ] adjusted easily to any changing technical demands, and in fact, would lead the effort to make some of these technology advancements to better serve the clients' needs. [   ] maintained an appropriate focus on areas such as scalability, supportability, compatibility, and robustness in any of [his/her] technology solutions. [S/he] kept current on all necessary certifications for the job and looked for additional certifications that could help [his/her] skill base.

[   ] skill level was such that [s/he] could address the most complex technical problems. [S/he] balanced the use of tactical versus strategic solutions in pursuit of the best resolution to a problem. [S/he] always designed technology procedures or solutions to be flexible, thus making them easily adaptable to future needs. [S/he] readily understood even the most sophisticated technical specifications and on [his/her] own produced extremely clear and easily understood technical documentation for use by others.

[   ] demonstrated a very high level of understanding of the business, which ensured that any technical skills would be applied to the real world and would not be relevant only in theory. [S/he] was able to communicate [his/her] technical visions to diverse audiences, from the most technical to those with a pure business mind-set.

[   ] abilities exceeded the level of technical skills required for the job, and in fact, [s/he] was regarded as an expert in several areas. [S/he] frequently assisted team members with their technical issues and readily shared information with the group on any technical matters of importance, particularly any changes in technology practices or trends. [S/he] quickly incorporated any applicable technological advances and helped the team with these advancements as well, often effectively overcoming any resistance to technical change.

TECHNICAL SKILLS
Downloadable Form 6.19 *(Continued)*

Specific examples of when [   ] showed exceptional technical skills were:

_____

_____

_____

_____

Met Expectations

[   ] met expectations in the area of technical skills over the past year. [S/he] demonstrated the appropriate level of understanding of the technical requirements of the job.

[   ] attempted to keep up-to-date on the technology aspects of the job. [S/he] took advantage of some technical trainings and occasionally would complete self-study activities. [S/he] kept current on all necessary certifications for the job. These efforts were typically completed in response to a particular technical need that arose on the job, rather than completed for proactive, visionary purposes.

[   ] demonstrated an average level of technical resourcefulness. [S/he] had several sources or procedures [s/he] would try in response to technical issues, which were often successful; however [s/he] would get stuck if they were not of sufficient assistance and in these instances would have to ask for help.

[   ] adjusted to several changing technical demands, although [s/he] did not take the lead in forecasting or implementing any of these changes. [S/he] maintained an appropriate focus on scalability, supportability, compatibility, and robustness in [his/her] technology solutions, although [s/he] could not always focus on all these factors in any given project. [S/he] understood most technical specifications and produced easily understood technical documentation for use by others.

[   ] attempted to keep an eye on the business needs in [his/her] application of technical skills. There were a couple of instances where [s/he] did not successfully navigate the divide between tactical and strategic solutions or the language of business vis-à-vis that of technology. For the most part, though, [s/he] was able to communicate [his/her] technical ideas to different audiences.

[   ] was not regarded as an expert in [his/her] technical abilities, however [s/he] was proficient in the skills needed for the job. In areas where [s/he] could help, [s/he] gladly assisted team members with their technical issues. [S/he] tried to

(continued)

TECHNICAL SKILLS
Downloadable Form 6.19 *(Continued)*

learn more about any technical advances, although [s/he] was not particularly proactive in gathering additional skills, nor was [s/he] at the forefront of anticipating or implementing any changes in technology practices or trends. Still, as these changes arose, [s/he] did not resist them and instead tried to incorporate them into [his/her] current practices.

Specific examples of when [   ] showed technical skills were:

_____

_____

_____

_____

_____

_____

_____

_____

Specific examples of when [   ] failed to show technical skills were:

_____

_____

_____

_____

_____

_____

_____

Did Not Meet Expectations

[   ] did not meet expectations in the area of technical skills last year. [S/he] did not demonstrate an understanding of the current technical requirements of the job, nor did [s/he] engage in behaviors in an attempt to improve [his/her] skills or knowledge.

[   ] did not keep up-to-date on the technology aspects of the job. [S/he] did not participate in any technical trainings or self-study activities over the course of the year. [S/he] either did not obtain or let lapse some of the necessary certifications for the job.

TECHNICAL SKILLS
Downloadable Form 6.19 *(Continued)*

[   ] resourcefulness in the technical aspects of [his/her] job was under par. If [s/he] was presented with a technical issue, [s/he] did not have the ability or motivation to try to solve it on [his/her] own. Instead, [s/he] would immediately ask for help from others on the team or in other technical areas. Even after the problem was resolved, [s/he] did not retain these learnings such that [s/he] could use the experience to deal with similar issues in the future.

[   ] had difficulty adjusting to changing technical demands and did not take the lead in forecasting or implementing any changes. [S/he] could not maintain the appropriate level of focus on areas such as scalability, supportability, compatibility, and robustness in any of [his/her] technology solutions. [S/he] could not understand complex technical specifications and also had problems producing technical documentation that could be clearly understood and used by others.

[   ] did not successfully consider the requirements of the business in [his/her] application of technical skills. [His/her] technical solutions tended to rely solely on tactical aspects, with no regard for strategic thinking. This resulted in solutions that were often good only for one situation and did not address broader business needs. [S/he] also had trouble communicating her technical ideas in a language appropriate to the audience—explanations were often too technology-focused for business audiences and too business-focused for technical audiences.

[   ] was never asked to assist team members with their technical issues. Instead, [s/he] tended to be the one doing the asking; this occurred repeatedly, even for the most basic technical issues or for those on which [s/he] had previously received coaching. [S/he] did not try to learn more about any technical advances, preferring instead to rely on outdated technology that [s/he] was familiar with. When technical changes were absolutely necessary, [s/he] adopted them only after great resistance.

Specific examples of when [   ] failed to show technical skills were:

_____

_____

_____

_____

_____

WORK HABITS*
Downloadable Form 6.20

Exceeded Expectations

[   ] exceeded expectations in the area of work habits last year. [S/he] missed very few days of work, planned [his/her] time off wisely, and was the model of punctuality for the group.

Over the past year, [   ] exhibited a stellar attendance record. You could count on [   ] being at work, and if [s/he] was not, it was for a serious and legitimate reason. [S/he] never missed work unexpectedly but rather would be sure to notify all appropriate parties. This included not only [his/her] manager and team members but also anyone [s/he] might come in contact with, including clients and members of other departments. [   ] made sure to provide these thorough notifications when [his/her] absences were planned as well as when any unscheduled absences came up . In all cases, [s/he] made sure to keep people in the loop about where [s/he] was, when [s/he] would be back, and who they could contact in the meantime. [   ] also frequently went the extra step and provided [his/her] backups with additional information [s/he] anticipated they could use.

[   ] was very thoughtful in [his/her] scheduling of time away from the office. [S/he] planned these absences well in advance in conjunction with the department schedule and made sure they did not put an undue burden on the department or on any of [his/her] coworkers. [S/he] spent the time to thoroughly brief everyone on work that would need to be done while [s/he] was away, including in these briefings information such as contact people, task, project outlines, and contingency plans.

[   ] made only proper use of break time. [His/her] breaks were never too long or too frequent and were always spent only on appropriate activities. When away from [his/her] desk, [s/he] could always be located on a moment's notice.

[   ] was a model of punctuality. [S/he] was always on time for meetings, and this punctuality applied whether it was a large, interdepartmental meeting or a small, one-on-one. Even more than being prompt, [s/he] frequently arrived several minutes in advance of the meeting or presentation. No event was ever delayed in waiting for [his/her] arrival. [   ] encouraged punctuality in others and engaged in activities to encourage this trend, such as making sure to start any meeting [s/he] facilitated promptly on time.

WORK HABITS
Downloadable Form 6.20 *(Continued)*

[   ] made sure not to waste other people's time. [S/he] always showed up to meetings fully prepared and ready to discuss all agenda items. When [s/he] led meetings or gave talks, [s/he] always made sure to finish on time. If the content of the meeting had not been completed, [s/he] would check with the group to see if they wanted to keep going, and if they could not, [s/he] would make plans to finish the meeting in another session.

[   ] was consistently one of the first people in the office in the morning and one of the last ones to leave at the end of the day. [S/he] was very organized and used [his/her] time well during the work day, always meeting and often beating deadlines. [His/her] impeccable work habits contributed to [his/her] exceeding [his/her] goals on a regular basis.

Specific examples of when [   ] showed exceptional work habits were:

_____

_____

_____

_____

_____

_____

_____

_____

Met Expectations

[   ] met expectations in the area of work habits over the past year. [S/he] missed an average number of days last year, attempted to plan [his/her] time off wisely, and strove for punctuality.

Over the past year, [   ] attendance record was unremarkable. You could typically count on [him/her] being at work, and if [s/he] was not, it was for a serious and legitimate reason. Only on rare occasions would [s/he] miss work unexpectedly, and if [s/he] did, [s/he] tried to notify all appropriate parties. [S/he] generally did a good job of this with [his/her] manager and team members but was not as thorough in updating others [s/he] might come in contact with (such as members of other departments and clients) that [s/he] was away. [   ] did a better job of providing these notifications when [his/her] absences were planned than

(continued)

WORK HABITS
Downloadable Form 6.20 *(Continued)*

when they were not scheduled. When [s/he] was away, [   ] kept people in the loop on basic information such as where [s/he] was, when [s/he] would be back and who they could contact in the meantime. [S/he] did not typically go the extra step to provide them with additional information [s/he] anticipated they could use.

[   ] tried to be thoughtful in [his/her] scheduling of time away from the office. [S/he] planned most absences in advance and in conjunction with the department schedule and checked that they did not put an undue burden on the department or on any of [his/her] coworkers. [S/he] sometimes misjudged [his/her] schedule, however, and planned to take off at inconvenient times or on last-minute trips, which did put a strain on [his/her] coworkers. Before being away, [   ] briefed people on work that would need to be done. In these briefings, [s/he] covered the basic information but did not always provide enough detail on contact people, task and project outlines, and contingency plans.

[   ] made proper use of break time. [His/her] breaks were appropriate in length, frequency, and activity. When away from [his/her] desk, [s/he] could typically be found quickly, although there were a few instances when [s/he] was needed and could not be located.

[   ] strove to be punctual. [S/he] aimed to be on time for meetings, and generally hit the mark, although not always. [S/he] tended to be more punctual at large, interdepartmental meetings or meetings where [his/her] presence was crucial (such as meetings [s/he] facilitated) than at smaller meetings or one-on-ones. [   ] was not a model of punctuality and typically did not arrive in advance of meetings or presentations; however, events were not usually delayed waiting for [his/her] arrival. [   ] tended to follow the punctuality level of the crowd rather than modeling punctuality on [his/her] own.

[   ] tried not to waste other people's time. [S/he] usually showed up for meetings fully prepared and ready to discuss the agenda items, although this preparedness could suffer if [s/he] was busy with other items. When [s/he] led meetings or gave talks, [s/he] tried to finish on time. [S/he] generally accomplished this, although there were several instances where the meeting ran over, and [s/he] let it go without checking with the group, causing inconvenient delays in other participants' schedules.

WORK HABITS
Downloadable Form 6.20 *(Continued)*

[   ] was not consistently one of the first people in the office in the morning nor one of the last ones to leave at the end of the day. However, there were situations where each of these cases was true. [S/he] attempted to be organized and use [his/her] time well during the workday, which resulted in [his/her] meeting most deadlines, although not by much. [His/her] solid work habits contributed to [his/her] meeting [his/her] goals on a regular basis.

Specific examples of when [   ] showed positive work habits were:

_____

_____

_____

_____

_____

_____

Specific examples of when [   ] failed to show positive work habits were:

_____

_____

_____

_____

_____

_____

(continued)

WORK HABITS
Downloadable Form 6.20 *(Continued)*

Did Not Meet Expectations

[   ] did not meet expectations in the area of work habits last year. [S/he] had issues with [his/her] attendance and time away from the office, and internally had problems with punctuality.

Over the past year, [   ] had a poor attendance record. [S/he] missed work on numerous occasions and exceeded [his/her] allotment of both sick and personal/vacation days. On several occasions, [   ] got in the pattern of missing work on a regular basis and in many instances, [s/he] did not provide legitimate reasons for [his/her] absences. Without warning, [   ] often would not show up for work, leaving coworkers continuously to wonder if [s/he] would be in on any given day. There were numerous times when people outside the group (other employees, clients, etc.) wanted to reach [   ] but could not because [s/he] was not in the office. [   ] did an extremely poor job letting people know that [s/he] was going to be out of the office. [S/he] made hardly any effort at all to do this when [s/he] was out unexpectedly—at times not even notifying [his/her] manager—but [s/he] did not do a much better job even with planned absences. Whether planned or unplanned, [   ] failed to update people on what [s/he] was working on and who could cover for [him/her] in [his/her] absence. This frequently had a negative impact on the progress of the projects with which [   ] was involved. [   ] also often failed to communicate the basic details of her time away from the office, such as if [s/he] could be contacted and how and when [s/he] would be back. [S/he] also failed to use crucial out-of-office messages on [his/her] e-mail and voice mail, again causing confusion and work slowdowns.

[   ] showed no planning or thoughtfulness in [his/her] scheduling of time away from the office. [S/he] failed to plan many of [his/her] absences in advance. [S/he] often asked for time off at the last minute and with complete disregard for what was going on with the department (e.g., if it was a busy time or other coworkers were on vacation). When [   ] did plan for absences, [s/he] failed to thoroughly brief everyone on work that would be needed to be done while [s/he] was away.

[   ] made improper use of break time. [His/her] breaks were frequently too long and too frequent and were often spent on personal activities. [S/he] often took breaks during the busiest part of the day. When away from [his/her] desk, [s/he] often could not be located, and this was true even when [s/he] knew that [s/he] may be needed for something.

[   ] also had problems with punctuality. [S/he] was never on time for meetings, and this lack of punctuality applied equally for large, interdepartmental meetings and one-

WORK HABITS
Downloadable Form 6.20 *(Continued)*

on-ones. [S/he] frequently walked in late to meetings and presentations, even when [his/her] presence was crucial and [his/her] lateness was disruptful; many events were delayed waiting for [his/her] arrival. [   ] lack of respect for punctuality frequently started a downward spiral where others would also be late. As a result, many meetings [s/he] facilitated or was involved in started significantly late.

[   ] actions often wasted other people's time. In addition to starting meetings late, [s/he] often showed up to meetings unprepared and not ready to discuss the agenda items. When [s/he] led meetings or gave talks, [s/he] consistently ran long, causing inconvenient delays in other participants' schedules. When these meetings ran over, [s/he] never checked with the group to see if they wanted to keep going but rather made the, often inappropriate, time decisions on [his/her] own.

Looking back over the past year, there were no examples of when [   ] was the first person in the office in the morning nor the last one to leave at the end of the day. As a rule, [s/he] put in the minimal amount of time necessary to get the job done and no more. In addition, [s/he] was often disorganized in [his/her] work and did not use [his/her] time well during the workday, which caused [him/her] to frequently miss deadlines. [His/her] poor work habits contributed to [his/her] failing to meet [his/her] goals on a regular basis.

Specific examples of when [   ] failed to show positive work habits were:

_____

_____

_____

_____

_____

_____

_____

_____

WORK MANAGEMENT*
Downloadable Form 6.21

Exceeded Expectations

[   ] exceeded expectations in the area of work management last year. Specifically, [s/he] excelled in the areas of time and project management, as well as planning, scheduling, and organizing.

Time Management

[   ] managed [his/her] time extremely wisely and productively last year. [S/he] set SMART (specific-measurable-achievable-realistic-time-bound) goals and then managed [his/her] time to effectively achieve those goals. [S/he] made good use of time management tools such as calendars, planners, time audits, and to-do lists. [S/he] used a formal process to manage [his/her] time and was always aware of the time management choices [s/he] was making. A key part of this was being able to assess the importance, urgency, and duration of any task, and [   ] did this unerringly. [S/he] used [his/her] time management process to keep [him/her] on track and started each day, week, month, and quarter with a set of goals or tasks [s/he] had to achieve. Then [s/he] used these goals and tasks to plan the activities [s/he] engaged in at any given moment.

[   ] prioritized [his/her] work effectively. [S/he] used [his/her] goals to set priorities and to avoid spending time only on areas that were urgent but not important in the long run, or, even worse, not important *and* not urgent. When competing priorities arose, [   ] assessed them carefully and always made the correct decision about which task or project to work on first and how to handle the others. [   ] strength at prioritization of work meant that [s/he] met, and often exceeded, all deadlines over the course of the year.

[   ] maximized the use of peak times throughout the day. [S/he] made effective use of any discretionary or downtime, such as travel, to continue to make progress on [his/her] goals. [   ] worked smarter not harder on [his/her] tasks. [S/he] did not get caught up in unnecessary details. [S/he] was able to multitask effectively and pace [him/herself] as needed to not lose momentum or burn out.

[   ] did not procrastinate in [his/her] work and handled distractions or interruptions well. [S/he] did not get caught up in time-wasting activities and eliminated any time snares [s/he] saw that were affecting the larger group. [S/he] also worked with colleagues and/or [his/her] manager to eliminate nonessential

tasks. [S/he] also worked to promote an atmosphere conducive to concentration and productivity. Every activity [   ] engaged in had a purpose. [His/her] working style was not so rigid that [s/he] could not be versatile, however. [His/her] time management process was flexible enough to bend successfully to any last-minute requests or crises [s/he] needed to address.

Finally, [   ] respected the time of others. [S/he] could give her manager or any interested party an update on [his/her] work at any time. [His/her] time management techniques were so strong, [s/he] coached others on those techniques. [His/her] colleagues knew that [s/he] was good for [his/her] word on timing—whether that meant showing up on time, presenting a deliverable on time, or not keeping others unnecessarily in meetings or conversations.

Project Management

[   ] exceeded expectations in managing projects last year. [S/he] excelled in all phases of project management from planning to executing to concluding.

[   ] displayed excellent abilities in project planning. [S/he] established clear project goals. [S/he] successfully used project planning tools and software. [S/he] created and implemented understandable project documentation to be used throughout the project. At the beginning of the project, [s/he] made accurate estimates of time and resources and organized these estimates into clear and detailed time lines, budgets, and resource requests. [S/he] also assessed the likelihood of any risks or obstacles that could arise over the course of a project and made plans on how to address them, should they occur.

During [   ] projects, [s/he] used these detailed plans to manage the day-to-day tasks and stay on track. If anything occurred that caused a delay, [s/he] ably adjusted the timeline and associated activities accordingly. [S/he] never let any of [his/her] projects go off course or stall indefinitely.

[   ] excelled at the people aspects of project management as well. For projects [s/he] managed, [s/he] selected the appropriate members for the team, assigned them to suitable roles, and worked well with all of them throughout the course of the project. [S/he] established a clear working methodology and communication plan to keep members in the loop and always knew where progress stood. [S/he] was extremely effective at motivating the project team and managing the interests and information needs of the projects' clients, sponsors, and stakeholders.

[   ] managed [his/her] projects so well that they were all completed on time or early and under budget. This was true even for the most complex projects or when [s/he]

(continued)

WORK MANAGEMENT
Downloadable Form 6.21 *(Continued)*

was balancing several projects at the same time. In concluding [his/her] projects, [s/he] always wrote comprehensive project reports, including clear findings and recommendations for future, related projects. [S/he] was able to present the key project deliverables in a succinct and impactful manner. [S/he] also conducted lesson-learned meetings, at which the team brainstormed strengths and developmental needs or "do wells" and "do differentlies" for current and future projects.

Planning and Scheduling

[   ] exhibited extremely strong planning and scheduling skills during the year. [S/he] balanced the long-term vision with the short-term actions. [S/he] successfully translated all these plans into reality, so they didn't just look good on paper but drove the actual work.

[   ] did this by developing sound and workable action plans. These plans were comprehensive and addressed every aspect and time frame of the work. [S/he] accurately assessed needs and anticipated reactions and addressed both as part of the planning process. [   ] plans addressed the strategic and the tactical needs as well as current and future needs.

[S/he] planned for the unexpected and had a contingency plan for any possibility that could arise. [S/he] called on a vast array of experiences and resources to overcome any delays and made sure to never be the cause of delays. [   ] never overcommitted [him/herself] or others, and scheduling conflicts that occurred were never of [his/her] doing.

[   ] scheduling skills shone in meetings. [S/he] planned meetings to best accommodate the schedules of those involved. [S/he] always respected time constraints by starting and finishing at the appointed hour. [S/he] made sure to have an agenda and used it to keep on track, manage speakers, and stay on target in the meeting.

[   ] recognized the need for success in planning and scheduling and therefore always made it a top priority. [S/he] never left it to the last minute and never inconvenienced others with [his/her] plans or schedules. [   ] model skills in these areas meant that others frequently relied on [him/her] to keep them organized and on task, which [s/he] did willingly.

WORK MANAGEMENT
Downloadable Form 6.21 *(Continued)*

Organizing

[   ] was extremely organized in [his/her] work. [S/he] was always on top of things and could put [his/her] finger on any piece of data—whether it be at [his/her] desk or on [his/her] computer—immediately. [S/he] never misplaced things but rather implemented an effective filing system and organizing tools that [s/he] used consistently. [His/her] workspace was the model of efficiency. [S/he] also displayed an organized approach to the tasks that [s/he] performed.

[   ] maintained this organization during times of crisis or stress. In fact, during these times, others consistently looked to [   ] to keep them organized and to keep the work under control while the problem was being addressed. This high level of organization helped [   ] stay highly productive and achieve all [his/her] goals over the course of the year. [His/her] organization also significantly contributed to the together impression of the entire department.

Specific examples of when [   ] showed exceptional work management skills were:

_____

_____

_____

_____

_____

_____

_____

_____

_____

_____

_____

_____

_____

(continued)

WORK MANAGEMENT

Downloadable Form 6.21 *(Continued)*

Met Expectations

[   ] met expectations in the area of work management over the past year. [S/he] performed at an average level in the areas of time and project management, as well as planning, scheduling, and organizing.

Time Management

[   ] managed [his/her] time well last year. [S/he] attempted to set SMART (specific-measurable-achievable-realistic-time-bound) goals and manage [his/her] time to effectively achieve those goals. [S/he] used time management tools such as calendars, planners, time audits, and to-do lists, although not always consistently. [S/he] attempted to use a process to manage [his/her] time, although this process was rather haphazard, and did not always successfully guide [his/her] time management choices. For example, [   ] attempted to use a process to keep [him/her] on track for each day, week, month, and quarter. However, [s/he] did not have a formal way to assess the importance, urgency, and duration of any task or a structure with which to list goals or tasks [s/he] had to achieve. This meant that [s/he] at times went off track managing [his/her] time and had to back up to refocus [his/her] tasks to achieve the objectives of the particular time period. Without this structure, it was somewhat hit or miss whether the activities [s/he] was doing were the correct, most effective ones.

[   ] prioritized [his/her] work effectively. [S/he] used [his/her] goals to set priorities, and while [s/he] knew that [s/he] needed to spend time on tasks that were important but not urgent, there were several times where [s/he] gave precedence to tasks that were urgent but not important in the long run, and the planning or development [s/he] intended to do suffered. When competing priorities arose, [   ] tried to make the correct decision about which to work on first and how to handle the others. [S/he] often did this well, but there were several times where [s/he] was influenced by the tasks others wanted done first, even if their assessment served only themselves and may have not been a true top priority. For the most part, though, [   ] prioritized accurately, which meant that [s/he] met most deadlines over the course of the year.

[   ] tried to plan [his/her] work during the day to maximize peak times. During these times, [s/he] was often able to work more productively, although there were instances where the extra work [s/he] was putting in was not necessarily the right work. At times [s/he] got caught up in detail, but [s/he] typically recognized when this happened and stopped to refocus. [S/he] showed evidence of an ability to multitask with easier tasks and usually paced [him/herself] as needed to not lose

momentum or burn out, although there were a few instances of working harder but not necessarily smarter that caused unnecessary stress.

[   ] tried not to procrastinate in [his/her] work. For the most part, [s/he] did not waste time, although [s/he] was better watching [his/her] own time than catching and changing any time wasters that were affecting the larger group. [S/he] was especially able to avoid procrastination when [s/he] liked or was motivated by a task. [S/he] struggled a bit more when the task was undesirable. [   ] handled most distractions and interruptions effectively. [S/he] recognized that [s/he] needed to work in an atmosphere conducive to concentration and productivity and tried to set up [his/her] environment in that way. There were occasions, however, when an interruption threw [him/her] off course, and [s/he] was not able to flex without sacrificing the completion of [his/her] primary task.

Finally, [   ] respected the time of others. [S/he] tried to only interrupt others from their work when necessary. [S/he] was also able to give her manager or any interested party frequent updates on [his/her] work status. [His/her] colleagues did not view [him/her] as the model time manager, but they knew that for the most part, [s/he] would manage to meet [his/her] deadlines without unnecessarily imposing on the time of others.

Project Management

[   ] met expectations in managing projects last year. [S/he] completed an average level of performance in all phases of project management from planning to executing to concluding.

[   ] displayed the ability to plan projects. [S/he] established project goals. [S/he] learned and used the basic project planning tools and software. [S/he] created and implemented project documentation. This documentation was meant to be used throughout the project, although at times it was either too detailed to be decipherable or too basic to be of any practical planning use. [   ] attempted to accurately estimate the time and resources needed for [his/her] projects, although these estimates were often somewhat off base and would have to be frequently revised. This affected the project time lines, budgets, and resource requests, which also were frequently under revision. [S/he] completed risk assessments as part of [his/her] project planning. These tended to be accurate as far as they went, but they often left out several important risks and fell short on offering feasible contingency plans for dealing with the issues, should they occur.

(continued)

WORK MANAGEMENT
Downloadable Form 6.21 *(Continued)*

[   ] always had good intentions of using [his/her] plans to stay on track and manage the daily activities of the project. [S/he] was successful in doing this if everything went according to plan. If anything occurred that caused a delay, however, [s/he] often had trouble and would need assistance adjusting the timelines and associated activities accordingly. There were times where without this assistance, [his/her] projects would have stalled indefinitely.

[   ] paid attention to the people aspects of project management as well. For projects [s/he] managed, [s/he] thought about selecting the appropriate members for the team and tried to assign them to roles best suited to their abilities and experience. [S/he] communicated frequently with the team, although there was no formal plan for these communications, which meant that sometimes team members felt out of the loop and had to find things out on their own. For the most part, people knew where the project progress stood, although again, when there were changes, [   ] lack of a plan with which to communicate these changes meant that some people were updated sooner than others. At times, this had a negative effect on the work. [   ] worked well with all team members. [S/he] tried to keep them motivated, although [s/he] failed to recognize the subtle needs of different team members in this regard. [S/he] did well at managing the interests and information needs of the projects' clients, sponsors, and stakeholders and only had to call in assistance for the most senior meetings or biggest crises.

[   ] managed [his/her] projects so that they met but did not go beyond expectations: They were done on time, but not early and were done on but not under budget. [S/he] struggled more with complex projects or when [s/he] had to balance several projects at the same time. When the projects were complete, [s/he] wrote project reports, covering all aspects of the current project. They were not always thorough, however, and did not address any strategic lessons learned, such as recommendations for future, related projects. [S/he] presented on the key project deliverables in a clear and accurate manner. Overall, [s/he] was not considered to be an inspired project manager, but [s/he] got the job done.

Planning and Scheduling

[   ] exhibited solid planning and scheduling skills during the year. [S/he] did a better job with short-term planning and scheduling than with long-term. Also, at times [his/her] skills were better in concept than in implementation.

WORK MANAGEMENT
Downloadable Form 6.21 *(Continued)*

[   ] tried to construct action plans for the work [s/he] did. These action plans tended to be mostly tactical. [S/he] would jump right in and say what needed to be done and how [s/he] was going to do it. [S/he] did not address as much the needs or goals behind the actions or attempt to anticipate problems and how to address them. This meant that the plans were often not as comprehensive or accurate as they could be, and they often had to be reworked "in the trenches." If delays arose, [his/her] plans were often not flexible enough to deal with them, and [   ] revisions often meant delays to other parties.

When [   ] planned meetings, [s/he] considered the schedules of those involved. [S/he] attempted to start and end [his/her] meetings on time, although there were several instances where [s/he] had to be reminded that it was time to wrap up. [S/he] usually provided an agenda for [his/her] meetings, although [s/he] was not as adept at subsequently using the prepared agenda to manage speakers and keep on track.

[   ] recognized the need for success in planning and scheduling but it was not always [his/her] top priority. Particularly in times of crisis or stress, [s/he] would abandon any formal planning process and instead simply react to the current problem. This haphazard planning could inconvenience others. [   ] tried to avoid this, and if [s/he] saw that things were consistently being done at the last minute, [s/he] would go to [his/her] supervisors and ask for help.

Organizing

[   ] was moderately organized in [his/her] work. [S/he] could track down requested data—whether it be at [his/her] desk or on [his/her] computer—although not always immediately. [S/he] had a filing system and organizing tools that [s/he] used, albeit inconsistently. [His/her] workspace would fluctuate between organized or not, as [s/he] would let papers build up significantly but then devote a period of time to getting them all organized again. When a task was presented to [him/her], [s/he] tried to approach it in an organized fashion, or at least thought about it.

[   ] did not always maintain [his/her] organization goals during times of crisis. [His/her] productivity tended to dip a bit in these times, although [s/he] was typically able to recover enough to meet most of [his/her] goals over the course of the year. [His/her] organization style did not establish the "together" impression of the department, but it did not detract from it either.

(continued)

WORK MANAGEMENT
Downloadable Form 6.21 *(Continued)*

Specific examples of when [   ] showed strong work management skills were:

_____

_____

_____

_____

_____

_____

_____

Specific examples of when [   ] failed to show strong work management skills were:

_____

_____

_____

_____

_____

_____

_____

Did Not Meet Expectations

[   ] did not meet expectations in the area of work management last year. [S/he] performed at a below-average level in the areas of time and project management, as well as planning, scheduling, and organizing.

WORK MANAGEMENT

Downloadable Form 6.21 *(Continued)*

Time Management

[   ] did not manage [his/her] time well last year. [S/he] did not seem to understand or use goals as the basis for controlling [his/her] time. When [s/he] did attempt to set goals, they did not follow the SMART (specific-measurable-achievable-realistic-time-bound) format, and thus were ineffective as guides to help [   ] manage [his/her] time to effectively achieve those goals. As a rule, [   ] did not use time management tools such as calendars, planners, time audits, and to-do lists, or used them inconsistently. On [his/her] own, [s/he] did not use a process to manage [his/her] time, and when [s/he] was instructed to do so, the results were entirely unsuccessful. [S/he] was incapable of coming up with a way to systematically manage tasks on a daily, weekly, monthly, or quarterly basis. When presented with a task to do, or even just at the start of a regular workday, [s/he] did not have a way to assess the importance, urgency, and duration of a task or list of things to do. As a result, [   ] would tend to start with the first task that crossed [his/her] path, regardless of how crucial it was. And as there was no structure, the minute another task arose that seemed more important, or even just more interesting, [   ] would often leave the first task uncompleted and move on to the next task. This haphazard method to managing time and tasks had numerous negative repercussions on the group's workflow, the planning of others, and the successful meeting of deadlines.

[   ] did not prioritize [his/her] work effectively. [S/he] did not use goals as the basis for [his/her] priority-setting process, so [s/he] had no way to judge whether a task was important or not or urgent or not. [S/he] prioritized far too many tasks based simply on their perceived urgency, often as presented inaccurately by others. Even worse, many of these tasks were not crucial to the work [s/he] needed to be accomplishing, and [s/he] would at times get stuck on tasks that were neither important nor urgent. When competing priorities arose, [   ] made decisions based on faulty criteria, such as which person was screaming louder for the deliverable or simply which task [s/he] felt like working on at that moment. This poor ability to prioritize meant that [   ] missed many deadlines over the course of the year.

[   ] made no effort to try to match the work that needed be done with the best time to complete that work. [S/he] seemed to have no peak time for [his/her] work, being slow to get started in the morning and then petering out quickly in the afternoon. [S/he] never took advantage of any downtime, such as travel time, choosing to use these breaks for private interests rather than to get ahead on any of [his/her] work tasks. When [   ] did find a way to put in extra effort on a task,

(continued)

WORK MANAGEMENT

Downloadable Form 6.21 *(Continued)*

---

inevitably it was a case of working harder but not smarter. On several occasions, [s/he] labored for hours on the wrong task, only to have to go back and redo all the work, causing an extreme amount of wasted time. [   ] was always getting caught up in the level of detail of a task, again wasting time on unimportant specifics. [S/he] showed no ability to multitask, but had to work on tasks sequentially. [His/her] poor work management style meant that there were several instances when [s/he] did not pace [him/herself] and either lost momentum or burned out.

[   ] was well known as an extreme procrastinator with [his/her] work. When given a task to do, [s/he] would find thousands of things to do before actually getting started. [S/he] frequently wasted time in two ways: (1) [S/he] would spend far too much time on personal activities, such as phone calls, e-mails, or surfing the Internet; (2) [s/he] would work on nonessential tasks such as making labels or organizing [his/her] contact list, when a far more pressing task was at hand. This procrastination worsened if it was a task that [   ] particularly disliked, and [s/he] continued [his/her] delay tactics even when given direct feedback to work on the requested task. [   ] also failed to handle distractions and interruptions well. [S/he] was highly susceptible to distractions from incoming phone calls or e-mails, visits by colleagues, and so on. For any of these activities, [s/he] would immediately stop working, attend to the distraction and often not return to [his/her] primary task for several hours. [S/he] also created too many of [his/her] own distractions, such as taking frequent time out to work on personal projects. [   ] also took an inappropriate amount of breaks. These could range from numerous trips to the kitchen or bathroom to more significant breaks such as long lunches or trips away from the office. In each of these instances, the time management of the task or project [s/he] was involved in suffered greatly.

Finally, [   ] was not only a poor manager of [his/her] own time, [s/he] also had no respect for the time of others. [S/he] frequently interrupted others during their work and often overstayed [his/her] welcome when [s/he] stopped by with an update or to ask a question. If [s/he] asked a question of a coworker, such as "Do you have a minute?" [s/he] would not even listen to the response and instead would simply charge ahead with [his/her] speech or request. When others asked [him/her] about the status of [his/her] work, [s/he] either went on for way too long and gave too much detail or had no ability to answer accurately. Overall, [   ] was viewed as someone who would most likely miss or ignore any deadlines for work [s/he] was given.

WORK MANAGEMENT
Downloadable Form 6.21 *(Continued)*

Project Management

[   ] did not meet expectations in managing projects last year. [S/he] displayed below average level of performance in all phases of project management from planning to executing to concluding.

[   ] displayed no ability to successfully plan projects. [S/he] would establish only the most general project goals. [S/he] struggled to use even the most basic project planning tools and software and often had to get external help in these areas. The project documentation [s/he] created was usually incomplete and frequently inaccurate. This documentation was meant to be used throughout the project, but usually it either included too many unnecessary details or was at too general a level to be of any practical planning use. [   ] was particularly unsuccessful at accurately estimating the time and resources needed for [his/her] projects. Almost any estimate [s/he] set at the beginning of a project would have to be significantly revised later on. These revisions negatively affected the project time lines, budgets, and resource requests for the project. [S/he] sporadically completed risk assessments as part of [his/her] project planning. When [s/he] did this exercise, the risks [s/he] included were only the most obvious ones, and even for these, [s/he] offered up only the most basic contingency plans.

[   ] did a poor job in managing the daily activities of [his/her] projects. As [his/her] plans were so faulty, there were no solid foundations to control the day-to-day tasks. [S/he] struggled to stay organized on a regular day, and if any unexpected problems or delays occurred, it was even worse. [S/he] had difficulty in flexing time lines or other plans to deal with changing circumstances. In fact, there were several times where [   ] projects came to a total halt, and without external assistance to get them back on track, they would have completely failed.

[   ] paid little attention to the people aspects of project management as well. For projects [s/he] managed, [s/he] chose [his/her] team members either randomly or based on irrelevant factors, such as who [s/he] liked the best. [S/he] had no communication plan for the team, so team members were always feeling out of the loop regarding what other people were doing or where the project stood in general. [S/he] did not schedule regular project meetings to be used for crucial discussions or announcements. [   ] did not work equally well with all team members. [S/he] had [his/her] favorites and let them know it, thus creating resentments on the team. [S/he] failed to recognize the importance of motivating the team or keeping up morale. When interpersonal issues arose among team members, [s/he] ignored them at all costs or gave advice to the employees to work it out among themselves. [S/he] did not do much better in dealing with the

(continued)

external people involved in [his/her] projects. [S/he] frequently failed to keep clients, sponsors, and stakeholders updated on key developments in the project and failed to get buy-in from some of these key groups when needed.

Overall, [   ] project management was significantly under par. Projects under [his/her] leadership more often than not missed important deadlines, including final deadlines, and came in way over budget. This was the case with even the most mundane of projects and was even worse with more with complex projects or when [   ] had to balance several projects at the same time. When [his/her] projects were finished, [s/he] often failed to complete final project reports, thus hampering the efforts of others to gather any lessons learned from [his/her] experience and increasing the chance that other groups working on similar projects in the future would have to start from scratch. When asked, [   ] was unable to present the results of the key project deliverables in a clear or accurate manner. Overall, [s/he] was considered to be an ineffective project manager.

Planning and Scheduling

[   ] exhibited poor planning and scheduling skills during the year. [S/he] struggled with short-term planning and scheduling as well as with long-term. When [s/he] made the effort to plan for something in advance, the plans typically failed in implementation.

[   ] rarely constructed action plans for the work [s/he] did. [S/he] tended to just jump right in at any part of the job with no planning for timing or resources. [S/he] never considered the needs or goals behind the actions and made no attempt to anticipate problems and how to address them. This meant that [his/her] plans often were not comprehensive or accurate, resulting in the need for numerous changes in the implementation phase. These changes meant that [   ] had a difficult time dealing with any unanticipated delays, and at the same time, [his/her] inefficiency in planning often resulted in delays to other parties.

[   ] was particularly notorious regarding [his/her] poor planning with meetings. When [s/he] chose the time for the meeting, [s/he] rarely considered the schedules of others involved, choosing instead the time that worked best for [him/her] (even if this was late on a Friday or in the middle of another company event). [S/he] never started or ended [his/her] meetings on time, missing these starting and ending points consistently. [S/he] rarely created an agenda for [his/her] meetings, and when [s/he] did, it included only the most cursory of details and was never used to manage the time of the meeting or keep people on track.

WORK MANAGEMENT
Downloadable Form 6.21 *(Continued)*

[   ] failed to recognize the need for success in planning and scheduling in [his/her] work. [S/he] had no particular process for planning, and any plan [s/he] attempted to implement, [s/he] would abandon instantly in times of crisis or stress in favor of reacting to the current problem. This haphazard planning frequently inconvenienced others, as they attempted to make their plans and schedules. [   ] paid no attention to this and consistently failed to recognize how [his/her] failures in the area of planning and scheduling had long-term effects on important strategic goals.

Organizing

[   ] was completely unorganized in [his/her] work. If [s/he] was asked for a piece of data—whether it be at [his/her] desk or on [his/her] computer—she inevitably would have difficulty putting [his/her] finger on it. [S/he] had no semblance of a filing system and made no attempt to use organizing tools, such as labeled files, planners, etc. [His/her] workspace was always extremely cluttered, and even though [s/he] claimed [s/he] could find things on it, no one else would have had a chance, not to mention that the visual appearance alone suggested a completely scattered employee. [   ] approach to work mirrored the appearance of [his/her] desk. When [s/he] was given a task to complete, [s/he] approached it in a completely disorganized fashion, just jumping in wherever [s/he] felt like with no regard for organizing a process or system. This lack of organization was consistently dire but got worse during busy times or during a crisis. [His/her] organization style was so bad that it detracted from the "together" image of the overall department.

Specific examples of when [   ] failed to show strong work management skills were:

_____

_____

_____

_____

_____

_____

_____

_____

Four Managerial Competencies

CHANGE MANAGEMENT*
Downloadable Form 6.22

Exceeded Expectations

Last year, [   ] exceeded expectations in the area of change management. [S/he] excelled in both dealing with changes that were presented to her and also driving through and communicating [his/her] own changes to staff and others.

[   ] was open to the idea of change. When presented with a specific change to adopt, [s/he] started by always making sure [s/he] understood everything about the change—who was proposing it, what the goal and reason for it was, what they thought it would improve, and all the impacts of the change. Once [s/he] gathered this information, and it met with [his/her] approval, [s/he] became a complete advocate for the change. [S/he] was very flexible in responding to change, even when it had to be done quickly. This was true for both small- and large-scale change.

If for some reason, [   ] had an issue with an element of the change, [s/he] would never shut it down immediately. Instead, [s/he] would work with the proposing parties to better understand their interests and reasons for the change. Often this would result in all parties gaining a better understanding of the change, and from that understanding, they would make minor adjustments to ensure the change worked for everyone.

When [   ] proposed change him/herself, [s/he] handled this process with great finesse. [S/he] never tried to force change down people's throats, but would spend a significant amount of time explaining the change in terms that were familiar and applicable to different audiences. [S/he] always investigated the impact of [his/her] proposed change on different parties and made sure to have answers on how to address these impacts when [s/he] communicated about the change. [S/he] listened and responded to any questions or concerns about [his/her] proposed change from others and always tried to secure buy-in from all parties before implementing change.

[   ] did an excellent of explaining changes to [his/her] staff. [S/he] always provided extensive details about the change, how it would affect individual workers and what the overall reason, context, and goals were for the change. [S/he] set a highly positive tone for all change, and as such, the staff always felt comfortable suggesting new ideas to [   ] . This open-to-change atmosphere resulted in the staff working together to suggest and implement numerous changes over the past year that resulted in significant improvements.

(continued)

CHANGE MANAGEMENT
Downloadable Form 6.22 *(Continued)*

As change was being implemented, [   ] offered extensive support to the staff. [S/he] was always aware of the effects that uncertainty could have on the staff's morale or production and as such worked to try to maintain an element of stability in the group during times of change.

In summary, [   ] was very open to the idea of change, always opting for something new if it was well-thought-out and reasonable, and would provide an improvement over the status quo. [   ] maintained this positive approach to change management whether the change was [his/her] idea or not, and for both short, quick changes as well as for longer, more strategic changes. Because [   ] positively managed these new circumstances, all the changes [s/he] implemented last year were successful.

Specific examples of when [   ] showed exceptional change management were:

_____

_____

_____

_____

_____

_____

_____

Met Expectations

[   ] met expectations in the area of change management over the past year. [S/he] met the basic requirements both in dealing with changes presented to [him/her] and in implementing [his/her] own changes to staff and others.

[   ] was generally open to the idea of change. When [s/he] was presented with a specific change to adopt, [s/he] asked questions and did research to try to understand more about the change. She attempted to find out who was proposing the change, what the goal and reason for it was, what they thought it would improve and the impacts of the change, although sometimes [his/her] questions in this regard were superficial, resulting in [him/her] getting only half of the story. Once [s/he] gathered this information, [s/he] usually got behind the change. It was harder for [   ] to process change if [s/he] needed to do it quickly. In these cases,

[s/he] tended to resist that change. Also, [s/he] was more flexible with small-scale changes that [s/he] understood than with more complex, large-scale changes.

When [   ] proposed change him/herself, [s/he] attempted to gather the proper buy-in. [S/he] didn't force change down people's throats, but would spend time explaining the change to different audiences. This was more effective with audiences with which [   ] was familiar and with whom [s/he] spoke the same language. [S/he] had more trouble explaining the change to and getting buy-in from audiences who questioned or pushed back on the change.

[   ] listened and responded to any questions or concerns from others about [his/her] proposed change. [S/he] often had not thoroughly done [his/her] homework on the impact of [his/her] proposed changes on different parties, which hampered [his/her] ability to effectively address these questions and concerns. [   ] did try to explain any changes to [his/her] staff. [S/he] always provided details about the change, including how it would affect individual workers and what the overall reason, context, and goals were for the change. Again, though, at times [s/he] did not include all these details in [his/her] communication plan, resulting in confusion or more questions on the part of the staff. On the whole, though, [   ] set a fairly positive tone for all change, and as such the staff felt comfortable suggesting new ideas. This open-to-change atmosphere resulted in the staff working together to suggest and implement a few successful changes over the past year. There were some instances, however, where [   ] shot down suggestions of change from the staff, even though in retrospect they would have resulted in improvements.

As change was being implemented, [   ] offered support to the staff. [S/he] was aware of the effects that times of uncertainty could have on the staff's morale or production. Other than being aware, however, [s/he] did not do much to try to maintain an element of stability in the group during times of change.

In summary, [   ] was relatively open to the idea of change. [S/he] proposed some changes [him/herself] and tried to implement these effectively. [S/he] managed change imposed by others fairly well, but did a much better job of this if it was something [s/he] understood and believed in and if [s/he] had time to process it.

(continued)

CHANGE MANAGEMENT
Downloadable Form 6.22 *(Continued)*

Specific examples of when [   ] showed strong change management were:

_____

_____

_____

_____

_____

_____

_____

Specific examples of when [   ] failed to show strong change management were:

_____

_____

_____

_____

_____

_____

_____

Did Not Meet Expectations

[   ] did not meet expectations in the area of change management last year. [S/he] had problems dealing with changes on [his/her] own and also had problems communicating changes to staff.

When change occurred over the past year, [   ] went one of two ways in managing it—both unsuccessful. In some instances, [s/he] was wholly opposed to change. [S/he] would not attempt to understand why the change was needed, and even if it was completely obvious that it would bring improvements, [s/he] resisted it and even actively tried to stop it. On the whole, [s/he] showed no flexibility in responding to changes, and this was true for both small and large-scale change.

At other times, if it was a change that [s/he] wanted or that would benefit him/her, [s/he] would attempt to push the change through, without regard to the effects or wishes of others. If others resisted this style of change management, [s/he] either

CHANGE MANAGEMENT
Downloadable Form 6.22 *(Continued)*

ignored them or told them just to "get on board." [S/he] never attempted to get buy-in for [his/her] desired changes. [   ] exhibited these behaviors even if [s/he] was proposing large-scale change. [S/he] showed no understanding of the possible implications in completely uprooting processes, procedures, or staff and just pushed people to make it happen. When [s/he] was able to get these changes implemented, the results on the other end were always disastrous.

When [   ] was forced to adopt a change that [s/he] did not want, [s/he] did so with great reluctance. [S/he] did a terrible job of explaining these changes to [his/her] staff. If she tried to explain the change at all, [s/he] did it in a cursory manner, providing few details about the change, how it would affect individual workers, or what the overall reason, context, or goal was for the change. [S/he] made sure that everyone knew that [s/he] was opposed to the new way of doing things. [S/he] set a negative tone for all change, and as such the staff felt completely reluctant to suggest anything new to [   ], even if these ideas would have offered significant improvements.

Once the change was being implemented, [s/he] offered little to no support to the staff. [S/he] seemed unaware of any effects times of uncertainty were having on the staff's morale or production. [   ] did nothing to try to maintain an element of stability in the group during times of change.

In summary, [   ] was very closed to the idea of change, always voting instead for the status quo. The only exception to this was when the change was of [his/her] doing, and in these cases, [s/he] did a terrible job of implementing [his/her] desired changes to achieve successful results.

Specific examples of when [   ] failed to show strong change management were:

_____

_____

_____

_____

_____

_____

_____

_____

LEADERSHIP*

Downloadable Form 6.23

Exceeded Expectations

[   ] exceeded expectations in the area of leadership. [S/he] led the team by example, and [his/her] leadership example was an exceptionally strong one. [   ] showed [s/he] was always ready to step up and take the lead.

[S/he] consistently operated under strong leadership principles that were known to everyone. This included treating everyone fairly and respectfully at all times. [S/he] inspired others to hold these same standards for themselves and was quick to give feedback and make necessary adjustments when these standards were not met. [S/he] was also able to adapt [his/her] leadership style to best deal with different circumstances, situations, and people.

Over the past year, [   ] created an inspiring vision for the group that was aligned to the department's and company's goals. [S/he] communicated this vision repeatedly to the team and used it to show how each individual's work made vital contributions to the team. This served as a powerful motivator. [S/he] constantly promoted this vision to the team and used it to create a shared purpose, providing common grounding to everyone's daily tasks.

[   ] showed an understanding for the strategic goals of the department and the company and drove [his/her] team to achieve them. [S/he] initiated advances in strategy and worked to develop a shared vision across the firm. [S/he] constantly reached out to other business groups to collaborate across company divisions. [s/he] effectively promoted the work of [his/her] team to others.

[   ] made communication an essential part of [his/her] leadership role. [S/he] always updated people immediately on developments that affected them and on larger company or departmental planning. During times of change or uncertainty, [s/he] communicated more than usual and did everything possible to provide stability to the team. [S/he] was a decisive leader and communicated [his/her] decisions quickly. [S/he] used participative leadership as appropriate and was always open to hear the ideas from members of [his/her] team.

[   ] also led by highlighting the successes of the team. [S/he] was quick to celebrate wins and always acknowledged the efforts and achievements of others. People were exceedingly proud to work for [   ] and were very loyal to [him/her]. [S/he] pushed people to raise the bar on what they expected from

---

LEADERSHIP
Downloadable Form 6.23 *(Continued)*

themselves and made sure to notice when they delivered. [S/he] was aware of the strengths of the team and fostered these strengths, and at the same time offered development assistance for areas of improvement. [s/he] maintained [his/her] support of the team during any setbacks and was not a leader only during the good times. In fact, [   ] leadership style shone most strongly during tough times. The team knew [s/he] could be relied on, and [his/her] confidence in success was contagious throughout the group. [S/he] took total responsibility for the group's performance.

In general, [   ] was perceived as a charismatic and trusted leader. [S/he] was seen as a role model for other developing leaders who frequently consulted [him/her] for advice. [S/he] inspired others through [his/her] words and actions and got the best out of [his/her] team. [S/he] was respected and listened to and commanded authority, although [s/he] used this authority to motivate and encourage rather than to dictate and punish. The overall feeling in [   ] group last year was one of excitement and optimism, and these feelings translated to high success rates in achieving their business goals.

Specific examples of when [   ] showed exceptional leadership were:

_____

_____

_____

_____

_____

_____

_____

_____

_____

_____

(continued)

LEADERSHIP
Downloadable Form 6.23 *(Continued)*

Met Expectations

[   ] met expectations in the area of leadership over the past year. There were several times where [s/he] stepped up to take the lead. In these instances [s/he] led the team by example, and this example was a good one.

[S/he] developed and communicated solid leadership principles. [S/he] treated people fairly and respectfully and encouraged others to do the same. When people on the team were not performing up to par, [s/he] gave feedback to redirect them, although sometimes [s/he] was not as quick as [s/he] should have been to recognize these problem situations. [   ] displayed a fairly consistent leadership style that others understood. However, [s/he] seemed unable to always adjust this style to deal with different circumstances, situations, or people, but rather would act in [his/her] leadership comfort zone, even if this was not ideal.

Over the past year, [   ] attempted to create a vision for the group. This vision considered, but was not explicitly aligned to, the department's and company's goals. [S/he] communicated this vision to the team and showed how it applied to each individual's work. [S/he] did not, however, consistently use this vision to inspire and motivate the team throughout the year, nor did [s/he] use it to create a shared purpose. For the most part, [   ] stayed within the confines of [his/her] group for the work [s/he] did on vision and strategy. [S/he] showed an awareness of the larger strategic goals of the department and the company but did not aggressively promote or work to integrate [his/her] vision or goals with this strategy. [S/he] did not significantly advance any work on strategy.

[   ] communicated what was necessary as part of [his/her] leadership role. [S/he] updated people on developments that affected them and on larger company or departmental planning, although not always in a timely manner. [S/he] was also slow in making some decisions and following up to communicate them to the team. During times of uncertainty, [s/he] recognized the need to increase communication and succeeded in doing this. [S/he] was not exceedingly confident in these communications, however, so that they did not provide an overwhelming feeling of stability to the team during times of change. In general, [   ] was open to hearing new ideas from members of [his/her] team.

Over the past year, [   ] highlighted many of the team's successes. [S/he] celebrated wins and acknowledged the efforts and achievements of others. People did not have problems working for [   ]. [S/he] expected people to deliver on their commitments but did not push them to raise the bar on their performance. [S/he] was aware of the general strengths and weaknesses of the team and made

LEADERSHIP
Downloadable Form 6.23 *(Continued)*

attempts to address them. Overall, though [   ] demonstrated a stronger leadership style in good times than in bad. If setbacks occurred, [s/he] had a tendency to either push them off on someone else or take over the whole operation and shut down any team input. [S/he] was not always viewed as a reliable leader when times got tough, and this lack of confidence affected the success of the group, as they knew that they might not always get the support they needed when problems arose.

In general, [   ] was perceived as a trusted leader. [S/he] was willing to share [his/her] leadership experiences when asked for advice and seemed interested in learning more about leadership. [S/he] was mostly consistent in [his/her] words and actions and aimed to get the best out of [his/her] team. [S/he] was respected and listened to, although more so on a case-by-case basis and when [s/he] had a particular expertise on a topic. [S/he] did not automatically command authority but was not ignored as a leader either. The solid level of leadership skills [   ] displayed contributed to [his/her] group meeting, although not exceeding, most of their business goals.

Specific examples of when [   ] showed strong leadership were:

_____

_____

_____

_____

_____

Specific examples of when [   ] failed to show strong leadership were:

_____

_____

_____

_____

_____

(continued)

Did Not Meet Expectations

[   ] did not meet expectations in the area of leadership last year. [His/her] guidance of the team was a poor example of leadership, and there were numerous times when [s/he] shirked [his/her] leadership duties entirely.

[   ] did not operate under any consistent leadership principles; if [s/he] had any, they were not conveyed to the team. There were several instances where [his/her] actions went against the most basic leadership ideals, including times when [s/he] treated people unfairly and with a lack of respect. Rather than inspiring, [his/her] leadership style was often offensive or demotivating at best. [S/he] tended to dictate rather than lead and was unable to adjust [his/her] leadership style to deal with different circumstances, situations, and people. [His/her] leadership behavior generated numerous complaints from team members, as it swung from being overly authoritarian to being completely absent.

Over the past year, [   ] failed to create an inspiring vision for the group. [His/her] version of a vision was made up of poorly defined directions on various tasks or projects that arose for the team. There was no statement of big picture thinking that aligned to the department's or company's goals. There was no attempt to explain how each individual's work contributed to the success of the team or to create a shared purpose. [His/her] staff performed their daily tasks as if they were working in a silo, with no information from the outside world. This severely hurt the motivation and production levels of [   ] team.

[   ] showed no understanding of the strategic goals of the department and the company. [S/he] made no attempt to initiate any advances in strategy or look for synergies across the firm. [S/he] showed no interest in reaching out to other business groups for collaboration, even when it was made clear that such collaborations were expected and necessary for advancement. [S/he] did not promote the work of [his/her] team to others.

[   ] leadership communication skills were extremely ineffective. [S/he] frequently failed to update staff on developments that affected them or on larger company or departmental planning. [His/her] staff often complained that they were the last to find out any announcements. During times of change or uncertainty, [   ] actually shut down communication, saying that [s/he] did not want to tell [his/her] staff anything until [s/he] got more information. This caused feelings of great insecurity among team members. [   ] was an indecisive leader and did not communicate any decisions [s/he] made quickly. [S/he] rarely used

LEADERSHIP
Downloadable Form 6.23 *(Continued)*

participative leadership and did not encourage team members to contribute ideas on any matter, preferring instead to hand down dictates and enforce them.

[   ] rarely highlighted the successes of the team. [S/he] often only celebrated efforts and achievements after they were pointed out by others, and in these acknowledgments, the team usually received only a basic comment such as "good job," with no further detail. [   ] staff did not report being proud to work on [his/her] team and were not loyal to [him/her]; on the contrary, many of [his/her] staff wanted to transfer to work somewhere or for someone else. [   ] seemed completely unaware of the strengths of the team and did nothing to foster these strengths. [S/he] seemed a little more aware of the team's weaknesses, but tended to complain or yell about these rather than offer any development assistance. When setbacks occurred for the team last year, [   ] provided no support, and in fact, any leadership [s/he] had been providing, seemed to vanish. During these tough times, the team knew [   ] could not be relied on. [His/her] lack of confidence in the success of the group was contagious, and in fact, they frequently failed in these situations. When they failed, [   ] took any steps possible to avoid responsibility for the failure, instead putting it all back on the team.

In general, [   ] was perceived as a poor leader. Neither [his/her] staff nor peers showed great trust in [his/her] ability to lead the team to success. [S/he] failed to inspire others through [his/her] words or actions and most assuredly did not get the best out of [his/her] team. [S/he] was not respected and this lack of respect meant that [s/he] was rarely listened to as a credible voice in important matters. [S/he] fluctuated between acting with unmerited confidence and complete indecisiveness. When [s/he] perceived [s/he] had authority, [s/he] typically used it with a heavy hand to force [his/her] team to act in accordance with [his/her] wishes. In other instances, even when [his/her] direction was crucial, [s/he] failed to act with any leadership at all. The overall feeling in [   ] group last year was one of pessimism and low morale, and these feelings translated to low success rates in achieving their business goals.

Specific examples of when [   ] failed to show strong leadership were:

_____

_____

_____

_____

MANAGING OTHERS*

Downloadable Form 6.24

Exceeded Expectations

[   ] exceeded expectations in the area of managing others. Specifically, [s/he] excelled in the areas of coaching and developing, delegating, and giving feedback, including performance appraisals.

Coaching and Developing

[   ] did an excellent job coaching and developing [his/her] employees last year. [S/he] displayed an acute awareness of the strengths and development needs for each of [his/her] staff. [S/he] provided continuous support and guidance to [his/her] employees, both when asked and when [s/he] saw a need. In these meetings, [   ] employees reported walking away with sound, practical advice they could use immediately as well as with inspirational words of wisdom that they could consider for the future. [S/he] addressed each problem by starting in a listening mode and asking lots of open-ended questions to make sure [s/he] understood the issues completely. Then [s/he] would guide the employee to come up with solutions on [his/her] own first and follow these up with suggestions based on [his/her] experience. If an employee had excelled at something, [s/he] would always celebrate it and encourage more of the same behavior. [S/he] consistently encouraged employees to raise the bar and tackle new challenges. [S/he] kept [his/her] employees' career development goals in mind and matched them with experiences designed keep them in the direction of achieving those goals. [   ] knew exactly who the high potentials were in [his/her] group and groomed them for future advancement in the firm.

[   ] made sure that all [his/her] employees had thorough, specific development plans. [S/he] frequently trained others on the job and also helped the staff generate developmental ideas on their own. [S/he] viewed training sessions and other development opportunities as crucial and encouraged employees to take advantage of as many learning opportunities as possible, within the constraints of the job responsibilities. There were numerous occasions when [s/he] voluntarily set up developmental opportunities for the staff, either for particular individuals (e.g., introducing them to someone for their network) or for the team as a whole (e.g., team development events). [S/he] encouraged ongoing self-development, modeled this, and rewarded extra effort in this area. [S/he] assigned tasks according to team members' talents and desires, which [s/he] always had a current

handle on. [S/he] helped employees learn from their experiences and apply their learnings to future situations. Overall, [s/he] was extremely involved in staff development and communicated strongly that [s/he] wanted only the best for [his/her] team.

It was frequently reported that [   ] was an excellent listener. When [his/her] employees approached [him/her] to discuss something, [s/he] would put aside [his/her] own tasks and give [his/her] full attention to the other person. [S/he] knew that an important part of [his/her] job was managing others, and [s/he] treated the responsibility as just that, not as an annoyance. [   ] maintained an open-door policy and always made [him/herself] available to staff.

Delegating

[   ] demonstrated the ability to delegate successfully last year. [S/he] knew when and what to delegate and struck the correct balance between giving enough work to empower an employee but not so much that the person felt overwhelmed.

[   ] would make a plan before delegating work. [S/he] organized the available work to assess which tasks were the most appropriate for delegating and which staff were the most appropriate recipients. [S/he] chose tasks to delegate based on valid reasons (such as helping an employee's development) and not simply because [s/he] found the tasks unpleasant, boring, or difficult. [S/he] used delegation to motivate and develop and not simply out of convenience.

When [   ] gave staff work to do, [s/he] always ensured they had the resources needed to succeed. For initial delegation, [s/he] assigned discreet, limited tasks and made sure the employee could handle these before assigning more complex tasks. [S/he] always set specific goals for the delegated work to ensure both [s/he] and the employee could evaluate if the delegation was successful. If the employee needed training before being ready to handle the new tasks, [   ] made sure [s/he] received this training. [S/he] also made [him/herself] readily available for questions. [S/he] identified backups for the person to whom [s/he] assigned the work and consistently checked in to see how things were proceeding after the initial delegation.

[   ] used cases where [s/he] was extremely busy while other team members were idle or when [s/he] was spending large amounts of time on tasks below [his/her] level as perfect times to delegate. [S/he] did this because it was good both for staff development as well as for the achievement of the task, and [s/he] would delegate in these situations, even if it meant giving up some work that was highly visible.

(continued)

[S/he] was not proprietary about [his/her] work but assigned tasks in the way that was best to get them successfully completed. Once [s/he] delegated, [s/he] did not micromanage [his/her] employees, but set them up with the tools needed for their success, made [him/herself] available for questions at all times, and left them alone.

Giving Feedback (including performance appraisals)

[   ] exceeded expectations in [his/her] feedback practices last year.

[S/he] set clear goals for [his/her] staff at the beginning of the year. These goals served as a solid base from which to link [his/her] performance feedback. [S/he] consistently followed and exceeded all the best practices in giving feedback: [S/he] gave the right amount of feedback—never overwhelming the employee with too much and always providing feedback when it was called for. [S/he] balanced the feedback—it was never exceedingly negative nor falsely sugarcoated around the main message. [   ] feedback was never misinformed or inaccurate; [s/he] based it only [his/her] own observations and not on secondhand reports. [His/her] feedback was specific—it included clear, behaviorally based examples of what the employee did and should continue to do or do differently. Finally, [   ] feedback always had the right timing—it was delivered soon after the event and in an appropriate environment.

After [   ] gave feedback, [s/he] checked in to see that the employee had proper awareness and acceptance of the feedback. [S/he] helped the person formulate a clear plan on how to take action on the feedback. [S/he] partnered with the employee to ensure successful change following the feedback, which meant that most of [his/her] feedback evoked change the first time around. When this happened, [   ] made sure to catch the employee doing something right and provide recognition for it. When this did not happen, [   ] was extremely effective in redirecting the behavior from what had happened to what was desired.

[   ] was especially skillful in delivering difficult messages. [S/he] recognized these situations as a crucial place for feedback and never avoided them, even though that was the easier course. When [s/he] delivered these messages, [s/he] did so in a descriptive not judgmental way, with a focus on support and development rather than on accusation and blame. [S/he] never personally attacked the other employee with [his/her] words. In delivering this feedback, [   ] dealt with defensiveness from employees well. [S/he] expected defensiveness and would plan for it, so [s/he] did not get emotionally hooked and reply with harsh words or other negative, unprofessional reactions. [S/he] was always open to listening to the other party's response to the feedback and

MANAGING OTHERS
Downloadable Form 6.24 *(Continued)*

incorporated this response into the action plan for the feedback, when possible. This was an effective method, which resulted in successful behavioral change due to [   ] feedback. In addition, [   ] tact in delivering difficult feedback never hurt and in fact improved working relationships with the staff going forward.

[   ] also performed at the highest levels in doing performance appraisals. [S/he] recognized that these reviews were a crucial part of performance management and put significant effort into their writing and delivering. [S/he] was on time or early with all [his/her] reviews, and each one was extremely thorough and detailed. [   ] had gathered lots of documentation on [his/her] staff's performance over the course of the year, so [his/her] appraisals included numerous rich, detailed examples. They focused on specific behaviors for the employee to develop or change and included a clear development plan going forward. All [   ] evaluation meetings went well, leaving [his/her] employees clear about their goals for the next year and motivated to achieve them.

In addition to success in these areas, [   ] handled other basic managerial functions perfectly. [S/he] closely monitored all employee administration, such as absenteeism, tardiness or time off, none of which were abused by many of [his/her] employees. [S/he] managed conflict quickly and well, catching and dealing it with early so it did not cause broader problems among the staff. Finally, [s/he] successfully motivated each member of the team to a successful meeting of their goals.

Specific examples of when [   ] showed exceptional management of others were:

_____

_____

_____

_____

_____

_____

(continued)

Met Expectations

[   ] met expectations in the area of managing others over the past year. Specifically, [s/he] met expectations in the areas of coaching and developing, delegating, and giving feedback including performance appraisals.

Coaching and Developing

[   ] spent time coaching and developing [his/her] employees last year. [S/he] was aware of the broadest strengths and development needs for each of [his/her] staff. [S/he] provided support and guidance to [his/her] employees, mostly when asked but also at times when [s/he] saw a need. [His/her] advice focused more on sound, practical tips than on sharing inspirational words of wisdom for the future. [S/he] tended to coach and develop by suggestion and could have spent more time up front in a listening mode to ensure [s/he] understood the issues completely and to prompt the employee to come up with solutions on [his/her] own first. If an employee excelled at something, [s/he] recognized it and encouraged more of the same behavior. [S/he] kept [his/her] employees' career development goals in mind and attempted to match them up with experiences designed keep them in the direction of achieving those goals. [   ] identified the high potentials in [his/her] group but did not take actions to specifically groom them for future advancement in the firm.

[   ] made sure that [his/her] employees had development plans. [S/he] relied on external training and development support as the resources for these plans. [S/he] saw value in training sessions and other development opportunities and encouraged employees to take advantage of a certain amount of these. On a few occasions, [   ] voluntarily set up developmental opportunities for the staff. [S/he] encouraged self-development but did not provide specific examples or models for this. [S/he] kept team members' talents and desires in mind when assigning tasks and encouraged employees to learn from their experiences, although again, this was often through words only, not with actions. Overall, [s/he] was involved in staff development and communicated that [s/he] wanted [his/her] team to improve.

[   ] exhibited solid listening skills. When [his/her] employees approached [him/her] to discuss something, [s/he] usually put aside [his/her] own tasks and gave [his/her] attention to the other person. There were examples, however, where [s/he] treated [his/her] responsibility of managing others as more of an inconvenience than a responsibility and crucial part of [his/her] job. This usually happened when [   ] was working under high personal stress. [   ] maintained an open-door policy and usually made [him/herself] available to staff.

Delegating

[   ] demonstrated the ability to delegate last year. For the most part, [s/he] knew when and what to delegate and tried to balance giving enough work to employees to empower them but not so much that they felt overwhelmed.

[   ] did not necessarily make a plan before delegating work. [S/he] knew as a manager that [s/he] needed to pass off some of [his/her] tasks, but [s/he] tended to delegate based on reasons of convenience rather than after thoroughly planning which tasks were the most appropriate for delegating and which staff were the most appropriate recipients. [S/he] recognized that delegation would help an employee's development but did not necessarily pick tasks to do that. Still, [s/he] did not delegate simply because [s/he] found a task unpleasant, boring, or difficult.

When [s/he] gave staff work to do, [   ] tried to ensure they had the resources needed to succeed. [S/he] answered questions and set up any needed training at the beginning of the delegation process but did not necessarily ensure that long-term support was in place. [S/he] did not set specific delegation goals but tended to pass off entire projects and evaluate the success of the delegation by the overall success of the project.

During the year, there were instances when [   ] was extremely busy while other team members were idle, or when [s/he] was spending large amounts of time on tasks below [his/her] level that [s/he] should have delegated and did not. [S/he] recognized the need for delegation in these instances but got so caught up in the current structure that [s/he] hesitated to change it. Still, when directed to do so, [s/he] did delegate effectively in these situations. [S/he] was not excessively proprietary about [his/her] work. Once [s/he] delegated, [s/he] tried not to micromanage [his/her] employees, although [s/he] did do this somewhat in projects that were highly visible.

Giving Feedback (including performance appraisals)

[   ] met expectations in [his/her] feedback practices last year.

[S/he] set goals for [his/her] staff at the beginning of the year and mostly used these goals as the base from which to link [his/her] performance feedback. [S/he] attempted to follow best practices in giving feedback and made it FAST: frequent, accurate, specific, and timely. [S/he] did not always accomplish all these standards in one instance of feedback (e.g., sometimes she gave feedback based on hearsay or feedback that was too vague or too long after the event), but [s/he] aspired to these standards.

(continued)

MANAGING OTHERS
Downloadable Form 6.24 *(Continued)*

[   ] helped [his/her] employees formulate an action plan for their feedback. These action plans were at times not specific enough. At times there may have been problems with the employee really having an awareness of or accepting the message, which meant that some of [   ] feedback did not evoke the desired changes the first time around. When this happened, [   ] tried to redirect the behavior from what had happened to what was desired and usually helped the employee to get it right after several tries.

[   ] struggled more with delivering difficult messages and tried to put off doing these as long as possible. [S/he] never personally attacked the other employee with [his/her] feedback in these situations, but [s/he] did not deal well with defensiveness from employees. [S/he] frequently got emotionally hooked and let the feedback message get off course and into a conflict situation. [S/he] started out with the desire to listen to the other party's response to the feedback but this listening would get shut down if [s/he] felt the employee was not immediately accepting the feedback, and [   ] would switch to sharply telling the person what to do without discussion. These situations hurt working relationships between [   ] and the staff for a period of time, although [s/he] would recognize this after the fact and work to smooth over any issues.

[   ] did what was expected in regard to performance appraisals. [S/he] recognized that these reviews were an important part of performance management and put effort into their writing and delivering. [S/he] was on time with the majority of [his/her] reviews and provided some specific details for each of [his/her] staff. [   ] had gathered some documentation on [his/her] staff's performance over the course of the year, so [his/her] appraisals included behavioral examples, although there could have been even more to supplement some of the general statements [   ] made about performance. All of [   ] reviews included a basic development plan. Most of [   ] evaluation meetings went well, although [s/he] did struggle with appraisals that required delivering tough messages.

[   ] handled other basic managerial functions successfully. [S/he] paid attention to employee administration, such as absenteeism, tardiness, or time off, and there were no major problems in these areas. [S/he] managed conflict as necessary, although [s/he] could have caught some of it earlier. Finally, [s/he] spent time attempting to motivate the team as a whole to be successful.

MANAGING OTHERS
Downloadable Form 6.24 *(Continued)*

Specific examples of when [   ] showed strong management of others were:

_____

_____

_____

_____

Specific examples of when [   ] failed to show strong management of others were:

_____

_____

_____

_____

Did Not Meet Expectations

[   ] did not meet expectations in the area of managing others last year. [S/he] performed at a below average level in the areas of coaching and developing, delegating, and giving feedback including performance appraisals.

Coaching and Developing

[   ] did not properly coach or develop [his/her] employees last year. [S/he] did not display an acute awareness of the strengths and development needs for each of [his/her] staff. [S/he] did not give support or guidance to [his/her] employees on a voluntary basis but rather would only hold such meetings when requested by the employee. In these meetings, [   ] employees reported that [s/he] did not give either sound, practical advice or inspirational words of wisdom. Instead, [s/he] offered quick, cursory solutions to problems and considered the problem resolved after only one meeting. If an employee excelled at something, [s/he] would not celebrate it nor encourage more of the same behavior. [S/he] never encouraged employees to tackle new challenges when they were ready and seemed to adopt the untenable view that the staff would be happy to remain in their same roles forever. [S/he] did not identify any high potential in [his/her] group and did not groom anyone for future advancement.

[   ] did not put any sincere effort into forming development plans for [his/her] employees. [S/he] rarely trained others or helped them generate developmental ideas on their own. [S/he] viewed training sessions and other development

(continued)

MANAGING OTHERS

Downloadable Form 6.24 *(Continued)*

opportunities as unnecessary time away from the office and agreed to them infrequently and unwillingly. There were no instances of where [s/he] voluntarily set up developmental opportunities for the staff, either individually or for the team as a whole. [S/he] also did not encourage self-development and did not reward any instances of this. [S/he] did not try to assign tasks according to team members' talents or desires, nor did [s/he] attempt to help employees learn from their experiences and apply their learnings to future situations. [S/he] took a very detached and uninterested approach to staff or team development.

It was frequently reported that [   ] was not a good listener. Often when people approached [him/her] to discuss something, [s/he] would seem distracted with [his/her] own tasks and was not able to put these aside for the sake of the other person's interest. [S/he] did not practice an open door policy but rather made [him/herself] available to staff only on a limited basis. On the whole, [s/he] did not demonstrate an interest in the issues of others and treated the fact that [s/he] had to manage others as more a bother than a responsibility to be respected.

Delegating

[   ] did not successfully delegate in [his/her] role of manager last year. [S/he] did not seem to know when and what to delegate and would swing from the extremes of giving unreasonable amounts of work to an employee to not being willing to give up any work and trying to do it all on [his/her] own.

[   ] had no plan for delegating. [S/he] would not organize the work to assess which tasks were the most appropriate for delegating. Rather, [s/he] would typically delegate tasks [s/he] found unpleasant, boring, or difficult. [S/he] made no attempt to match the delegated tasks up with the correct staff to receive them. [S/he] did not delegate to motivate or develop but focused on delegating strictly out of convenience.

When [s/he] gave staff work to do, [   ] did a poor job of making sure they had the resources needed to succeed. For initial delegation, [s/he] did not assign discreet, limited tasks to employees but rather would often "dump" large, complex tasks on people. [S/he] did not set specific goals for the delegated work. [   ] did not offer training or support for any knowledge or skill gaps and did not make [him/herself] readily available for questions. [S/he] did not identify backups for the person to whom [s/he] assigned the work and did not check in to see how things were proceeding after the initial delegation.

There were also instances when it was obvious that [   ] should delegate tasks and chose not to. In some cases, [s/he] would be extremely busy while other team members were idle or [s/he] would spend large amounts of time on tasks below [his/her] level. Both of these situations called for delegation, but even though the staff was in the position to accept more tasks, [   ] would not delegate. This seemed to happen more when [s/he] felt the project [s/he] was working on was highly visible, and [s/he] did not want to pass any interesting work on to others. When [s/he] was forced to delegate in these situations, [s/he] did not empower the employees with the authority or resources needed to succeed, but rather required them to run all aspects of their work through [him/her], effectively negating any of the positive effects of the delegation.

Giving Feedback (including performance appraisals)

[   ] failed to provide feedback using good practices to [his/her] staff last year.

[S/he] did not set clear goals for [his/her] staff at the beginning of the year, so [s/he] did not have a solid base with which to link [his/her] performance feedback. [   ] made many mistakes when giving feedback: [S/he] gave the wrong amount of feedback—either way too much or none at all, when comments were called for; [s/he] did not balance the feedback—it was either so negative that it completely derailed the employee's motivation, or it was so positive that the employee did not receive the message of what [s/he] needed to change. At times, [   ] feedback was misinformed or inaccurate, usually because [s/he] had gotten the facts from a secondhand source; [his/her] feedback was usually vague—it did not include clear, specific, behaviorally based examples of what the employee did and should continue to do or do differently. Finally, [   ] feedback almost always had the wrong timing—it was either too rushed and not given the attention of a proper conversation, or it was too delayed, and [s/he] would comment on something to an employee weeks or even months after an event. There were also instances where [s/he] gave individual feedback in inappropriate places, such as in a team meeting or in front of clients.

After [   ] gave feedback, [s/he] did not check in to see that employees had proper awareness and acceptance of the feedback. [S/he] also did not help them formulate a clear plan on how to take action on the feedback. Given this, it was not surprising that most feedback that [   ] gave over the course of the year was not successful—the employee would either continue to do the incorrect or undesirable behavior, or, in the case of positive feedback, would not work to capitalize on the strength [s/he] had exhibited. In these cases, [   ] would be at a loss on how to redirect the behavior, and if the employee did get it right, [   ] did not recognize it, which meant the desired behaviors would fall away after a while.

(continued)

MANAGING OTHERS
Downloadable Form 6.24 *(Continued)*

[   ] particularly had trouble delivering difficult feedback. In negative feedback situations, [s/he] was more likely to not deliver any message at all. When [s/he] did deliver these messages, [s/he] did so in a judgmental way, with a focus on accusation and blame rather than on support and development. [S/he] did not deal with defensiveness from the other party well and would typically get emotionally hooked and reply with harsh words or other negative, unprofessional reactions. [S/he] was not open to listening to the other party's response to the feedback but just tried to get in, deliver the bad message and get out. This was an ineffective method, which meant that more often than not, the behavior that was the source for the difficult message did not change. [His/her] lack of tact in delivering difficult feedback also hurt working relationships with the staff going forward.

[   ] also performed poorly with regard to performance appraisals. [S/he] did not put proper effort into either the writing or delivering of these reviews. [S/he] was late on all of [his/her] reviews, and it was not due to adding too much detail to the evaluations, which were cursory at best. [S/he] had not gathered documentation on [his/her] staff's performance over the course of the year, so the appraisals lacked rich, specific examples. They did not focus on specific behaviors for the employee to develop or change and included no plan for improvement going forward. Many of [   ] evaluation meetings reportedly went off track, leaving employees either confused or upset.

In addition to problems in these areas, [   ] did not handle other basic managerial functions well. [S/he] did not closely monitor employee absenteeism, tardiness, or time off, and these areas were abused by many of [his/her] employees. [S/he] did not manage conflict well, and there were numerous examples of small problems among the staff ballooning into big ones, due to [   ] lack of speed in taking corrective action. Finally, [s/he] failed to motivate the majority of the team to meet their goals.

Specific examples of when [   ] failed to show strong management of others were:

_____

_____

_____

_____

STRATEGIC THINKING*
Downloadable Form 6.25

Exceeded Expectations

[   ] exceeded expectations in the area of strategic thinking last year.

[S/he] was completely knowledgeable about strategy at several different levels—the strategy of [his/her] own work, team, and department as well as that of other departments and the overall company. In [his/her] work, [s/he] kept focused on big picture thinking and the realization that the sum of all the parts is meant to come together to achieve a broader whole or goal. [S/he] did this by frequently stepping back to evaluate if the team was still on track and making tactical adjustments to meet larger strategic goals, as necessary. [   ] did not let short-term pressures distract [him/her] from longer-term objectives.

[   ] exhibited strategic thinking when [s/he] saw common threads between work going on in different groups and was able to link these threads for enhancement. [S/he] did this for resources, ideas, or work processes; whatever the topic, [   ] was able to see connections other people missed and use these connections to move the work ahead more productively, quickly, and successfully. [   ] was always on the lookout for strategic alliances that would make finding these connections easier. [S/he] had a quest for synergy and inspired others on [his/her] staff to look out for new ways groups could work together as well.

[   ] organized and prioritized work to match the strategic needs of the group. [S/he] thought strategically about [his/her] own workforce and made sure to line the right people up for the right roles. [S/he] realized how everyone's roles and functions came together and how actions by one group impacted others. [S/he] was also able to think strategically about changes that were occurring in areas such as production, marketing, or leadership and adjust [his/her] workflow accordingly. Finally, [s/he] exhibited strong strategic thinking about the competition and industry trends and used [his/her] vast knowledge in these areas to bring a perspective broader than just what was going on inside the firm to [his/her] ideas.

Not only did [   ] keep an eye on and help execute strategy, but [s/he] consistently contributed to forming the strategy for [his/her] group and staff. [S/he] identified what the key future needs were as stated by the company and set [his/her] own strategies accordingly. [S/he] then did an excellent job of vetting this strategic thinking with the appropriate parties and making sure it got woven

(continued)

in to the other relevant strategies. [S/he] clearly communicated all strategic guidelines to the team, as appropriate, and used these strategies to explain how everyone's work moved the broader goals of the company ahead.

Specific examples of when [   ] showed exceptional strategic thinking were:

_____

_____

_____

_____

_____

Met Expectations

[   ] met expectations in the area of strategic thinking over the past year.

[S/he] was knowledgeable about strategy at a few different levels, mostly dealing with [his/her] immediate areas or the most basic company strategies. In [his/her] work, [   ] kept an eye on the big picture and understood that different parts had to work together to achieve broader goals. [S/he] attempted to translate strategic goals into tactical operations. Often, [s/he] was successful in doing this when a strategy was newly in effect and very clearly communicated. [S/he] had more difficulty translating strategy into action when changes to the original plan needed to be made or when [s/he] did not understand the original strategy. At times, [   ] let short-term pressures distract [him/her] from longer-term objectives, although for the most part, [s/he] was able to correct [his/her] course later on.

[   ] exhibited [his/her] best strategic thinking when specifically directed to think in this manner. When asked to look at a situation strategically, [s/he] saw common threads between work going on in different groups and was able to link these threads. While the links were not typically the most innovative or inspirational, [s/he] was able to do this for several different topics. [S/he] fell short in coming up with connections that other people missed or that put forth a completely new idea, and as such, the result of [his/her] strategic thinking was to move the work of the group ahead, but not significantly. [   ] did try to find alliances that would make finding strategic connections easier. [S/he] understood the need for synergy and attempted to promote it among [his/her] staff.

STRATEGIC THINKING
Downloadable Form 6.25 *(Continued)*

At various points, [   ] thought strategically about [his/her] own workforce and tried to line the right people up for the right roles. [S/he] realized how everyone's roles and functions come together and how actions by one group affect others. Again, [s/he] did a better job of this strategic planning at the beginning of a project, than when strategic changes needed to be made down the line. [   ] organized work to match the strategic needs of the group and worked to prioritize tasks accordingly. On the whole, [   ] did a better job of strategic thinking regarding [his/her] own work and staff than on broader areas. [S/he] did not make an effort to understand the strategies of other groups or departments, which limited the reach of [his/her] strategy thinking.

In some instances, [   ] contributed to forming the strategy for [his/her] group and staff. [S/he] tried to link these strategies with what [s/he] understood were the future needs of the company and was able to accomplish this, at least at the most basic levels. [S/he] vetted this strategic thinking with the appropriate parties but was not proactive in asking about other groups' strategies and how they could be woven together to create more synergies. [S/he] communicated broad strategic guidelines to the team, as appropriate.

Specific examples of when [   ] showed strategic thinking were:

_____

_____

_____

_____

Specific examples of when [   ] failed to show strategic thinking were:

_____

_____

_____

_____

(continued)

STRATEGIC THINKING
Downloadable Form 6.25 *(Continued)*

Did Not Meet Expectations

[   ] did not meet expectations in the area of strategic thinking last year.

[S/he] either did not seem interested in thinking about the big picture or was not capable of thinking outside the immediate box of [his/her] current work. [   ] displayed no knowledge of the strategies of the company, other departments, or other teams and very little knowledge of the strategies in [his/her] own area. [S/he] did not seem to understand the link between how the successful performances of different individuals and groups combine to result in successful performance for the company. Instead, [s/he] showed more of a tendency toward silo thinking—doing [his/her] own thing in the short term without regard for longer goals. When [s/he] was forced to focus on longer-term goals, [s/he] was not able to maintain this focus for [him/herself] or [his/her] team, and the minute more immediate fires arose, [s/he] responded to them, often ending up very far away from [his/her] originally intended goal.

[   ] exhibited no strategic thinking in regard to the workforce. In [his/her] own staff, [s/he] made no attempt to match the right people up with the right tasks but rather assigned tasks on a random basis, without thinking of broader implications. Because [s/he] did not look for common threads between the work going on in [his/her] group and different groups, [   ] or [his/her] staff spent time reinventing the wheel, instead of capitalizing on these links and moving the work forward. [S/he] made no attempt to organize or prioritize work based on [his/her] strategy, choosing again to simply respond to the crisis of the moment. [S/he] had no strategic alliances with other groups either internal or external to the firm and seemed to have no desire to create them. The idea of finding synergy was not a motivation in [his/her] work, but rather [   ] considered finding connections between different groups or processes to be an unnecessary bother. When shown concrete examples of how strategic thinking contributed to advancements, improvements, and the achievement of goals, [   ] seemed uninterested or unable to translate these examples into any strategic thinking of [his/her] own.

Over the past year, there were no examples when [   ] contributed to the strategy for [his/her] group and staff. [S/he] did not attempt to link the work [s/he] and [his/her] work were doing to the overall goals of the company. [S/he] did not vet any planning ideas with other parties and showed no interest in asking others about their strategies or how their planning could be woven together. [S/he] rarely, if ever, communicated any big picture messages to [his/her] staff, choosing to focus on the immediate tasks at hand, but not why they were necessary or what they were meant to accomplish. [   ] staff frequently complained that they were

STRATEGIC THINKING
Downloadable Form 6.25 *(Continued)*

"at a loss" for understanding the basic reasons behind some of the work they did. And in fact, with the lack of a strategy, many of the staff's tasks were unorganized and unnecessary. This lack of a big picture, long-term, strategic focus had a large, negative impact on the motivation and production of [   ] staff last year.

Specific examples of when [   ] failed to show strategic thinking were:

_____

_____

_____

_____

_____

_____

William S. Swan, Ph.D., is president of Swan Consultants, Inc. Established in 1980, his firm makes research about proven methods and skills associated with the interview and performance appraisal processes available. This "Science behind the hiring process" is applied in the *How to Pick the Right People* Selection Interview Workshop, and the Campus Recruitment Interview Program. The *How to Do a Superior Performance Appraisal Program* is the performance management system.

A nationally recognized expert in interviewing and performance appraisal, Dr. Swan conducts seminars and workshops for major corporations and government agencies. He has personally trained over 100,000 managers to conduct more effective interviews and performance appraisals, and is the author of two major books. *Swan's How to Pick the Right People Program* covers the selection interview process and *How to Do a Superior Performance Appraisal* focuses on performance management. Both are published by John Wiley & Sons.

Dr. Swan is also Associate Dean, Executive and Professional Education, at the Peter J. Tobin College of Business, St. John's University.

Prior to establishing his own consulting firm, Dr. Swan was Senior Vice President at Drake Beam Morin and a senior trainer with the Psychological Corporation. There he designed and conducted training programs in selection interviewing, campus recruitment, and performance appraisal, as well as provided general consulting services to a broad range of clients—both in the United States and overseas.

Before joining Drake Beam Morin, Dr. Swan was the assistant dean of the New York School of Psychiatry and program director at Albert Einstein Medical Center and Kingsboro Psychiatric Center. He is a New York State licensed psychologist, and has served on the faculty of Temple University, Clarkson University, and John Jay College.

Dr. Swan served two terms as president of the New York Metropolitan Chapter of the American Society for Training and Development, and served on the chapter's board of directors. He is also a member of the

Society for Human Resource Management and the American Psychological Association.

Dr. Swan earned his doctoral degree in Clinical Psychology from Temple University, his master's degree from St. John's University, and his bachelor's degree from Manhattan College.

Leslie E. Wilson, M.S., is the president and founder of LEW Learning, a New York-based training and consulting firm. Through her work, she focuses on partnering with clients to achieve sizable and strategic advances in the areas of learning and personal/professional development. Ms. Wilson has broad experience in the field of learning and development and works with clients worldwide in a variety of industries. Her particular areas of expertise include leadership, team development, communication skills, performance and change management, facilitation, and training strategy.

Prior to starting LEW Learning, Ms. Wilson was the manager of professional skills development for UBS Financial Services, Inc. At UBS, she touched all aspects of the career and talent lifecycle for employees—from analysis to design/development, delivery, and the evaluation of learning programs. In this role, she led a team charged with overhauling the firm's open enrollment training offerings and ran a firm-wide performance management training program. She also facilitated numerous senior management meetings and managed a mentoring program for the firm.

Before joining UBS, Ms. Wilson worked at Goldman Sachs, Inc., where she was a senior project manager and trainer, again specializing in performance management and communications skills. Prior to Goldman Sachs, her work experience was focused on international human resources through a consultant role at ORC Worldwide and an account manager role at Ernst and Young, LLP.

Ms. Wilson has received numerous certifications from most of the well-known corporate training companies, including BlessingWhite, Personnel Decisions, Ridge Associates, and Myers-Briggs. She earned her M.S. in Industrial/Organizational Psychology from the Georgia Institute of Technology and her B.A. from the University of North Carolina at Chapel Hill. In addition to the United States, she has consulted with clients in Canada and Mexico, Europe and Asia and rates travel as one of her favorite hobbies.